r. 4.50

Facsimiles of the 1994 ceasefire statements: IRA, 31 August,
and Combined Loyalist Military Command, 13 October
(Courtesy of John Harrison Photography)

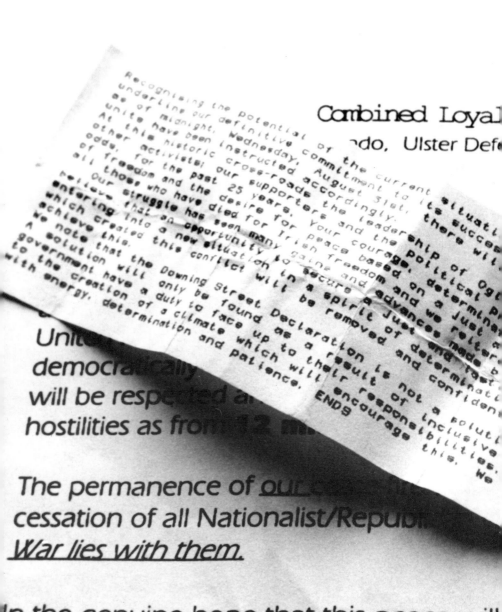

AUTHORISED

ilitary Command
ociation and Ulster Volunteer Force)

ed by representations from the Ulster
d after having received confirmation
titutional position within the
belief that the
in Northern Ireland
rational

order to enhance the democratic peace process and
lership of Oglaigh na h-Eireann have decided that
plete cessation of military operations. All our
h-Eireann salutes and commends our volunteers,
who have sustained this struggle against all
sacrifices have demonstrated that the spirit
ng settlement cannot be crushed, we remember
commitment to our republican objectives.
ilists and for the democratic position. We are therefore
ament has been created we are therefore
confidence and determined that the injustices
strength and justice of our struggle to
was it presented as such by its authors.
tions. Others, not least the British
our desire to significantly contribute
eryone to approach this new situation

ed

to

unity to
id the

ermand
s and Volunteers
The UNION IS SA

Brian Rowan was born in Belfast in 1958. After a period working as a freelance sports journalist, he became a subeditor with the *Sunday News* in 1981. In 1984 he founded the Ulster Press Agency with Jim McDowell and Joe Oliver and in 1987 became an independent freelance journalist, contributing reports and features to a wide range of outlets, including the BBC, the *Irish Times*, the *Irish Independent*, the *Irish News* and *Fortnight*. In 1989 he was contracted by the BBC as a specialist in the security field, and was appointed as Chief Security Correspondent in 1994. In the 1995 Institute of Public Relations Media Awards he was highly commended in the television news category and shortlisted for Reporter of the Year. He lives in Belfast and is married with two children.

BEHIND THE LINES

The Story of the IRA and Loyalist Ceasefires

BRIAN ROWAN

CHIEF SECURITY CORRESPONDENT, BBC NI

THE
BLACKSTAFF
PRESS

BELFAST

First published in 1995 by
The Blackstaff Press Limited
3 Galway Park, Dundonald, Belfast BT16 0AN, Northern Ireland

© Brian Rowan, 1995
All rights reserved

Typeset by Paragon Typesetters, Queensferry, Clwyd

Printed in Ireland by ColourBooks Limited

A CIP catalogue record for this book
is available from the British Library

ISBN 0–85640–564–7

for
Val, Ruairi and Elle

CONTENTS

PREFACE

Nineteen ninety-four was a truly remarkable year in Northern Ireland – a year in which both the IRA and the loyalist leaderships announced ceasefires. So, after twenty-five years of killing, the latest search for a political settlement is happening in an atmosphere of relative peace. On both the republican and loyalist sides the different violent organisations remain intact. They have not stood down their 'active service units' nor have they given up their weapons, and the so-called paramilitary 'punishment beatings' have continued. For these reasons the security approach to the changing situation has been cautious, but already there have been significant responses to the two ceasefires.

That the IRA was prepared to order a 'complete cessation of military operations' has much to do with the arguments that were put forward by Gerry Adams – the father of modern-day republicanism. In a briefing to the IRA leadership just before the ceasefire announcement he said he believed there was the potential to break 'the political, constitutional and military stalemate'.

The decision of the republican leadership to opt for a ceasefire was supported by their prisoners. On his release from jail in May 1995 Danny Morrison, one of the movement's principal strategists, said that support remained solid. In an article in the republican newspaper *An Phoblacht* on 1 June 1995, he was quoted as saying, 'No one is dissenting from the peace process and we accept there is a need for dialogue. People are unhappy, however, that the British are slowing the pace of the peace process and haven't engaged in meaningful dialogue. The view from the jail is that they [the British] hoped to put pressure on the IRA and wreck the peace process, but in being flexible the IRA has taken the moral high ground.'

Since the IRA ceasefire there have been exploratory talks involving the minister for political development at the Northern Ireland Office, Michael Ancram, and a republican delegation led by Martin McGuinness and also including Gerry Kelly. In Washington in May 1995 the Northern Ireland secretary of state, Sir Patrick Mayhew, held what was described as an 'informal meeting' with Gerry Adams. In these talks as in the exploratory discussions the British government says it was emphasising the need for IRA weapons to be 'decommissioned'. Republicans and loyalists have both insisted that the weapons issue can only be dealt with as part of an overall negotiated settlement, and Britain has yet to define precisely how this issue can be dealt with.

In the unfolding situation since the ceasefires Adams has also met the United States President Bill Clinton and two Irish prime ministers, Albert Reynolds and his successor, the Fine Gael leader, John Bruton. Loyalists too have been involved in talks with Michael Ancram and have been to the United States to put their case. All these remarkable developments would have seemed impossible a year ago, but there is now a momentum carrying the Northern Ireland peace process along.

The process that aims to carry Northern Ireland past the point of two ceasefires and closer to a permanent peace will be a slow one, for this is a place where people are still deeply suspicious of each other. Small, gentle steps will be required if the fragile peace is not to be damaged.

In this book I do not pretend to have the full story of how the two ceasefires were achieved, but *Behind the Lines* will put new material into the public domain and I hope it will contribute something to people's understanding of how the two cessations of violence were achieved. Many people have helped me with this book: Gerry Adams, Gusty Spence, Martin McGuinness, David Ervine, Gary McMichael, Albert Reynolds, the Revd Roy Magee, Sir Hugh Annesley, Cardinal Cahal Daly and Senator Gordon

Wilson (who died suddenly on 27 June 1995) are among those who agreed to speak to me on the record. So too did the SDLP leader John Hume and the Church of Ireland Primate Dr Robin Eames – two men who were of critical importance in the search for the breakthrough that finally came last year. There are others whom I would like to name but cannot, and I think of three people in particular who made an enormous contribution to this book. They will recognise their input and I thank them for all their help.

In my work with the BBC I have reported on some of the darkest days in the recent history of Northern Ireland – days when hope was nowhere to be found and human suffering was all too evident. Throughout those times Keith Baker, Tom Kelly, Pat Loughrey and Robin Walsh were hugely supportive: during the many difficult times when fine judgements had to be made I always knew I could depend on their backing. I have sought the advice of many other colleagues over the years, and I thank them all. I also want to thank Jim McDowell, who almost fifteen years ago gave me my first job in journalism; since then his support and friendship have been constant.

The hope is that the two ceasefires announced by the IRA and the Combined Loyalist Military Command in August and October 1994 will lead to something better for all the people of Northern Ireland. For the sake of my children, and your children and the next generation, let us hope so.

BRIAN ROWAN
28 JUNE 1995

A NEW DAY OF HOPE

31 August 1994: it would be a day of huge historic significance, a day twenty-five years into Northern Ireland's Troubles that would bring with it new hope of progress in a country so badly hurt by conflict. The horrific consequences of that violent quarter of a century can be measured by the death tally – a statistic that shows that more than three thousand people lost their lives on a long and painful journey to that August day. I remember the sun was shining as I made my way to work that morning, and not long into the journey I took a call on my mobile phone. I recognised the voice immediately and asked the taxi driver if he would mind pulling over to the side of the road. For the brief duration of the conversation I stood on the street and was given instructions to be at a rendezvous point in west Belfast at eleven o'clock that morning. By the time the call had ended – only a matter of seconds after it had begun – I was sure that the IRA, the Irish Republican Army, was just a couple of hours away from a ceasefire declaration. There was a certain inevitability about the occasion. Republicans had for some weeks been sprinkling the seeds of ceasefire speculation throughout the media, and the story on this historic August day was not just that the IRA would declare a ceasefire; really it had more to do with the ceasefire's precise terms.

When I arrived at the BBC in Belfast, I shared with a handful of my most senior colleagues the timing of the expected announcement. By 9.30 that morning, when several dozen journalists crammed into Keith Baker's office for the regular daily newsroom meeting he chaired as the BBC's Head of News and Current Affairs in Northern Ireland, there were about six people in the room who knew the importance of the ninety minutes that lay ahead. When this meeting broke up I was part of a much smaller gathering attended by Baker, his two most senior editorial deputies, Tom Kelly and Andy Colman, and Chris Cramer and Clive Ferguson from BBC National News; it was here that a plan of action was agreed. On receiving the ceasefire statement I would call Tom Kelly on his direct line, dictate the all-important lines of the declaration, and the BBC would then go on air with a newsflash. The long-suffering people of Northern Ireland would be given the news as soon as we had it.

Before then, however, there was more work to be done. By ten o'clock I was sitting across a table from a man who for several years had been my principal source within the loyalist camp. He had in-itiated this encounter and when we met, not far from the BBC building, he passed me a statement from the Combined Loyalist Military Command (CLMC) – a terrorist leadership with authority to speak on behalf of all the violent loyalist groups. They too were expecting an IRA ceasefire announcement and the statement he gave me was to be their initial reaction to it. I copied the statement and placed the notes in my pocket; later they would form part of the coverage of this momentous newsday.

The caller who had spoken to me as I made my way from my home in Holywood to work that morning had deliberately not used the name of the location I was to go to at eleven. In Northern Ireland there are many listening ears; reporters and their sources tend to be careful when speaking on the phone, and so I was simp-ly told to turn up at 'the same place' I had been the previous Satur-day. At around 10.40 on the morning of 31 August, I headed for west Belfast. At the meeting place I collected a cup of coffee and took a seat next to a woman who was alone. I had met the IRA's messenger here once before. That was some weeks earlier, when she had worn a short jacket and denims; today, however, she was dressed in a trench coat, blouse and skirt and she had taken a seat next to a window. When I sat down I noticed that a tiny piece of paper wrapped in clingfilm was resting on her lap, and as she unfolded it I could see it was the IRA statement which had been reduced to minute print. In whispered tones the woman began to read the declaration, and I copied it in a mixture of short- and long-hand. This particular statement was much too important to risk losing words in a rushed scribble.

The terms of the ceasefire came in the opening sentences: 'Recognising the potential of the current situation and in order to enhance the democratic peace process and underline our definitive commitment to its success the leadership of Oglaigh na h-Eireann [the IRA] have decided that as of midnight, Wednesday August 31st, there will be a complete cessation of military operations. All our units have been instructed accordingly...' These were remarkable words and I found it difficult to believe what I was hearing. Republicans had long argued that there would be no unilateral IRA cessation – no ending of IRA operations until there was movement by Britain on republican demands – but that was exactly what this statement was offering. The unexpected – I suppose even the unthinkable, given all that had been said in the past – had happened, and when those two opening sentences had been read I asked the woman if it would be possible for her to pause for a moment to allow me to ring them through to my news editor. My request was refused. The instructions that had been given to the messenger were to read the statement in full, and so I continued to note the declaration.

'...At this historic cross-roads the leadership of Oglaigh na h-Eireann salutes and commends our volunteers, other activists, our supporters and the political prisoners who have sustained this struggle against all odds for the past 25 years. Your courage, determination and sacrifice have demonstrated that the spirit of freedom and the desire for peace based on a just and lasting settlement cannot be crushed. We remember all those who have died for Irish freedom and we reiterate our commitment to our republican objectives. Our struggle has seen many gains and advances made by nationalists and for the democratic position. We believe that an opportunity to secure a just and lasting settlement has been created.

We are therefore entering into a new situation in a spirit of determination and confidence; determined that the injustices which created this conflict will be removed and confident in the strength and justice of our struggle to achieve this. We note that the Downing Street Declaration is not a solution, nor was it presented as such by its authors. A solution will only be found as a result of inclusive negotiations. Others, not least the British government, have a duty to face up to their responsibilities. It is our desire to significantly contribute to the creation of a climate which will encourage this. We urge everyone to approach this new situation with energy, determination and patience.' The statement was delivered with the codeword P. O'NEILL, the recognised stamp of authority of the IRA leadership.

As the woman walked away, I called Tom Kelly and read the opening sentences of the statement to him. For around twenty minutes or so he and Keith Baker had been waiting anxiously for me to call and now they had the words with which to make a historic news announcement. I told Kelly that the IRA had said there would be a complete cessation of military operations from midnight, all its units had been instructed accordingly and the IRA leadership had saluted and commended its volunteers. Within seconds, another of my colleagues, Donna Traynor, was reading these few short lines of copy in a newsflash on BBC Radio Ulster.

So, the waiting was over. Political reaction came flooding in, and in Dublin the Irish foreign minister and Labour Party leader Dick Spring called on loyalist paramilitaries to follow the example of the republican leadership: 'The republican leadership have made a courageous move. I would appeal to the paramilitaries on the loyalist side to recognise in turn the damage which their violence has inflicted on the whole community and on the ideals they claim to serve. They too have an opportunity now to end their violence. They can without loss of principle opt for the political path on their side also. I would echo what one loyalist representative said on television recently: if there is indeed a window of opportunity

4

and the chance to end violence, don't let unionists and loyalists be the ones to close it.'

The loyalist leadership, however, was not yet ready to match the IRA ceasefire. The statement I had noted before travelling to west Belfast that morning said the CLMC would not be dancing to a 'pan-nationalist tune', and it called on the main leaders of unionism, Dr Ian Paisley of the Democratic Unionist Party (DUP) and James Molyneaux of the Ulster Unionist Party (UUP), to seek a joint meeting with the British prime minister, John Major. Loyalists wanted to know if any secret deals had been done with the IRA, and they were also seeking guarantees about the future constitutional status of Northern Ireland. The statement meant that, for a while more at least, those who for twenty-five years or more had killed in the name of Ulster would continue to haunt its streets. Within hours of the IRA cessation of military operations, the Ulster Freedom Fighters (UFF) shot dead a young Catholic man in north Belfast, and in the weeks that followed, as the leaders of loyalism contemplated the future and their response to the republican ceasefire, there were many more acts of violence.

That response to the IRA ceasefire finally came on 13 October 1994, when the political representatives of loyalism staged a news conference at which they read a supplied statement from the CLMC. From midnight that night there would be a 'universal cessation of operational hostilities'. The people of Northern Ireland could at last breathe a sigh of relief: at last there was the hope of something better, something less violent, more peaceful. But there had been so much hurt along the way; the healing process was only just beginning and political differences were still, evidently, far from being resolved. Republicans had delivered their ceasefire in the belief that there now existed a favourable political climate in which their aims of a British withdrawal and an end to the partition of Ireland could be advanced, while the loyalist leadership had matched that cessation having been assured that the union with Britain was safe. Nevertheless, through the violent blur of the late eighties and early nineties it had been difficult to imagine that a breakthrough of any sort could be achieved. But away from Northern Ireland's killing field the political theorists in both the republican and loyalist camps had been considering an alternative path.

2

PEACE COMES DROPPING SLOW

Throughout the late 1980s and into the 1990s, with Northern
Ireland by now locked into its third decade of conflict, the IRA still
gave the impression of being an organisation in pursuit of some
sort of armed victory. But in the background significant things
were happening. Republicanism was undergoing a process of self-
scrutiny which would produce two documents: *A Scenario for Peace*
and *Towards a Lasting Peace*. Following talks between delegations
from the Social Democratic and Labour Party (SDLP) and Sinn
Féin in 1988, the respective party leaders John Hume and Gerry
Adams became involved in a secret dialogue, the detail of which
was being reported to the British and Irish governments by Hume,
and there were contacts between the British government and the
republican leadership. It would take time for all of this to create
the conditions for a better future but, to quote the words of the
poet W.B. Yeats, 'peace comes dropping slow'.

The first of the documents outlining a republican peace strategy,
A Scenario for Peace, was issued in May 1987; it was an indication
that while the IRA continued with its 'long war' the political
theorists within the republican movement were perhaps looking at
other possibilities. In a February 1994 article in the *Starry Plough*,
which is essentially an internal Sinn Féin magazine, one of those
theorists, Tom Hartley, said that *A Scenario for Peace* had emerged
out of 'the ongoing political debate that was taking place within
the party'. Hartley said that as a first public statement of Sinn Féin's
peace strategy the document had defined national self-
determination for Ireland in the context of international law, it had
addressed the issue of the unionists and their place in an Irish

democracy, and it had endorsed the principle that it was up to the Irish people as a whole to determine the future status of Ireland. But though Hartley described the document as a 'peace plan', it would not have made pleasant reading for unionists – indeed those living within that community would have viewed the document as nothing more than a raw statement of republican objectives – objectives that unionists would want nothing to do with.

The document described loyalists as a 'national minority in Ireland' and said that loyalism derived 'an artificial psychological strength from the British presence'. For its part, Sinn Féin was seeking a new constitution for Ireland which would include written guarantees for those 'presently constituted as loyalists':

> The resolution of the conflict would free unionists from their historic laager mentality and would grant them real security instead of tenure based on repression and triumphalism. We do not intend to turn back the pages of history, or to dispossess the loyalists and foolishly attempt to reverse the Plantation. We offer them a settlement based on their throwing in their lot with the rest of the Irish people and ending sectarianism. We offer them peace. We offer them equality. It is only through the process of decolonisation and dialogue that a peaceful, stable Ireland will emerge. Only when independence is restored can Ireland hope to prosper and take her place among the nations of the world. Britain must take the initiative and declare its intention to withdraw. That is the first step on the road to peace. Republicans will respond quickly and positively.

As part of what republicans were seeking, the document stated, 'a definite date within the lifetime of a British government would need to be set for the completion of this withdrawal'.

The document proposed 'free elections' to an all-Ireland constitutional conference. This would be made up of the elected representatives of the Irish people and would also be open to submissions from other significant organisations such as the trades union movement, the women's movement and the Churches. Its purpose would be to draw up a new constitution and to set out a national system of government. Loyalists would be given 'firm guarantees' of their religious and civil liberties. The document said that as part of a British military withdrawal the Royal Ulster Constabulary (RUC) and the Ulster Defence Regiment (the UDR, which was later to become the Royal Irish Regiment, RIR) should be disarmed and disbanded. All 'political prisoners' should be unconditionally released. In autumn 1994, in the post-ceasefire period, these demands were repeated by republicans as part of a package of demands on 'demilitarisation'.

As part of the proposals for a settlement that it outlined, *A Scenario for Peace* said that the British government 'must accept the responsibility for providing financial support by agreeing by treaty with the national government to provide economic subvention for an agreed period':

> Given the disastrous involvement of British rule in Ireland, reparations for an agreed period are the least contribution Britain could make to ensure an ordered transition to a national democracy and the harmonisation of the economies, North and South. Anyone unwilling to accept a united Ireland and wishing to leave should be offered resettlement grants to permit them to move to Britain or assist them to move to a country of their choice. The onus is on the British government to ensure a peaceful transition to a united and independent Ireland. The shape of that society is a matter for the Irish people. Only when Britain recognises that right and initiates a strategy of decolonisation along these lines will peace and reconciliation between Irish people and between Britain and Ireland be established.

Six months after the publication of that 'peace plan' the awful reality of the IRA's 'war' intruded on a most solemn occasion. In the late eighties there were many killings, but the Remembrance Day bombing in Enniskillen in November 1987 stands out from the many other horrors. Indeed, there is one reason in particular why that day of remembering will never be forgotten. In the aftermath of the explosion, despite the fact that eleven people had been killed, remarkable words of forgiveness emerged from the rubble surrounding the Enniskillen Cenotaph. Amazingly they were spoken by a man whose young daughter died that Sunday.

Gordon Wilson has told the story of that black and shameful November day many times, and when he spoke to me in Dublin – where he is now a member of the Irish Seanad – on 2 February 1995 his eyes were filled with tears. He is a man who understandably is still hurting but who carries no hatred for those who murdered his daughter. As our conversation began, he emphasised to me that he spoke as Marie Wilson's father and not on behalf of the other families who lost loved ones in the explosion. His story begins at the point where he was buried in the rubble with his young daughter.

'I asked Marie four or five times was she all right, and all the time holding my hand she assured me yes but each time and in between she screamed. I couldn't understand why on the one hand she was telling me that she was all right and on the other hand she screamed as dozens of other people were screaming and I knew something had to be wrong. I couldn't understand it and when I asked her for what was the last time, Marie, are you all right? she said, Daddy, I love you very much. Those were gorgeous words.' Gordon Wilson believes his daughter knew she was dying. Those were the last words she spoke to him and he remembers being driven home from hospital by his son Peter (who has since died), and saying to his wife Joan that 'the pet, as we called her' had told him that she loved him: 'And I cried like a child as I'm now doing.' Hours later, having been approached by a BBC producer whom he knew, Gordon Wilson gave an interview to Radio Ulster. He was asked in that interview about his feelings for those who had placed the bomb and his reply was interpreted in terms of forgiveness. When we spoke in Dublin, Gordon Wilson told me that although he had not used the word 'forgiveness' he had effectively forgiven his daughter's killers. He believes that Marie's last words had placed him on 'a plane of love', that her words had enabled him to think in terms of love rather than of hate.

Approaching six years after his daughter's death, Gordon Wilson would come face to face with representatives of the IRA leadership and would make a direct appeal for an end to violence. Meanwhile, in the period between the Enniskillen bombing and the August 1994 IRA ceasefire, many more families would suffer as the Wilsons had. The IRA's campaign would continue to rage and would once again spread into what one Special Branch officer described as 'three theatres of operation'; there would be attacks not only in Northern Ireland, but also in Britain (including the murder of the Conservative MP Ian Gow), and in other parts of Europe including killings in Germany, the Netherlands and Belgium. But in the background the seeds of a peace process were being planted.

A few months after the Enniskillen bombing, in a St Patrick's Day letter to the Sinn Féin president, Gerry Adams, on 17 March 1988, the leader of the SDLP John Hume said it was his belief that the violence of the IRA would not achieve its political aims. That letter formed part of the documentation exchanged between the SDLP and Sinn Féin in delegation talks in 1988. These talks, set up at the request of an anonymous third party, brought into the same room for a series of meetings some of the most senior figures and key strategists in both parties. Indeed, the make-up of the two delegations provides some indication of how seriously each party approached this project. The SDLP was represented by its two most senior members, John Hume and Seamus Mallon, and the delegation also included Austin Currie (who is now a Fine Gael representative in the Irish parliament), and Sean Farren. Sinn Féin was represented by party president Gerry Adams, party director of publicity Danny Morrison, and two of its foremost theorists, Mitchel McLaughlin and Tom Hartley. An internal party committee set up to monitor the talks included Martin McGuinness. It was out of these beginnings that a so-called 'Hume–Adams agreement' would eventually emerge in 1993. That agreement is at the heart of what republicans now call the 'Irish Peace Initiative' and in August 1994 Gerry Adams concluded that it provided the potential to break the 'political, constitutional and military stalemate'. His analysis was accepted by the IRA's Army Council, and so it could be argued that the 1988 talks between Sinn Féin and the SDLP formed the foundations on which a process leading to a ceasefire was built.

By the time those talks began, loyalist terrorists had successfully smuggled a huge arms consignment into Northern Ireland. The UDA leadership, meanwhile, was beginning to take a new shape. In December 1987 the IRA murdered John McMichael, one of the most prominent paramilitary figures in the loyalist camp, and three months later in March 1988 Andy Tyrie was ousted as UDA Supreme Commander in an internal coup. Some years down the road, both McMichael's son Gary and Tyrie would have roles to play as loyalists moved towards their ceasefire but in that period of the late eighties running through into the 1990s there would be a dramatic upsurge in the violence of both the Ulster Freedom Fighters (UFF), a cover name used by the Ulster Defence Association (UDA), and the Ulster Volunteer Force (UVF).

In those talks between the SDLP and Sinn Féin in 1988, the two parties were asked 'to explore whether there could be agreement on an overall nationalist political strategy for justice and peace'. In his St Patrick's Day letter to Gerry Adams, the SDLP leader outlined his analysis of the situation at that time and posed a number of questions. John Hume said it had already been admitted on all sides that there could be no military solution and he asked, 'Is it not time for the IRA and the members of the Provisional Republican Movement to seriously reconsider the methods that they have chosen to achieve their objectives or are they in danger of moving to a situation, or are they already in it, where the methods have become more sacred than the cause?'

With a view to creating conditions in which all military and violent activity could be brought to an end, John Hume then set out a number of questions:

1 Do you accept the right of the Irish people to self-determination?
2 Do you accept that the Irish people are at present deeply divided on the question of how to exercise self-determination?

3 Do you accept that in practice agreement on exercising that right means agreement of both the unionist and nationalist traditions in Ireland?

4 If you accept 1, 2 and 3 would you then agree that the best way forward would be to attempt to create a conference table, convened by an Irish government, at which all parties in the North with an electoral mandate would attend? The purpose of such a conference would be to try to reach agreement on the exercise of self-determination in Ireland and on how the people of our diverse traditions can live together in peace, harmony and agreement. It would be understood that if this conference were to happen that the IRA would have ceased its campaign. It would also be understood in advance that if such a conference were to reach agreement, it would be endorsed by the British government.

5 In the event of the representatives of the unionist people refusing to participate in such a conference, would you join with the Irish government and other nationalist participants in preparing a peaceful and comprehensive approach to achieving agreement on self-determination in Ireland? Would we in fact and in practice take up the challenge laid down by Wolfe Tone?

In reply, Sinn Féin said it accepted the right of the Irish people 'as a whole' to self-determination. The party said it recognised that unionists had 'democratic rights', but those rights 'must not extend to a veto over the national rights of the Irish people as a whole'. Sinn Féin also made clear in relation to the suggested conference that it wanted unconditional talks, that the precondition of an IRA cessation of operations should not be attached to the proposal.

Although you will acknowledge that we have not accepted without qualification 1, 2 and 3 we would, however, respond positively to the proposal for a round table conference. Obviously a conference of all Irish parties, not just those in the North, would be useful and attendance would pose no problem to Sinn Féin. However, we do not believe that such a conference would be the best way forward (it would only be part of the way forward) because it would be held

– as in your hypothetical question – in the absence of a prior declaration of intent to withdraw from Ireland by the British government. We must, however, reject any notion of having preconditions imposed on our attendance or on the attendance of any other party with elected representatives. *De facto* sovereignty over the two states of Ireland is exercised by the British and Dublin governments. Implicit in the exercise of Irish national self-determination is that the British government relinquishes its claim to sovereignty over the six-county state. Political, constitutional and psychological reasons, therefore, dictate that the British government be involved in any process which will realise the exercise of Irish national self-determination. A conference would of necessity have to be prefaced by an indication from the British government that it indeed intends to relinquish its sovereignty over the six counties. Irish reunification as a stated policy objective would constitute, as a first step, the minimum requirement of such an indication. In the absence of such a declaration, unionists assured by the veto conferred on them by the British government would feel no compulsion to move towards a consensus on the means to constructive British disengagement. Alternatively, they would simply decline the invitation to attend. We do not believe that a conference called by the Dublin government only can effect the desired objective of achieving the exercise of Irish national self-determination. Such a conference might prove useful in concerting steps for alleviating some of the abuses suffered by Northern nationalists and for obtaining international support for that end. Furthermore, a reaffirmation of pan-nationalist consensus on Irish reunification would prove particularly constructive if there was a follow-through in the form of seeking international support for that objective. But the problem would remain if neither the British government nor the unionists participated. For nationalists the key questions are how to get the British government to recognise Irish national rights; to change its present policy to one of ending partition and the union within the context of Irish reunification and, having done so, how we secure the co-operation of a majority in the North to the means of implementing those rights.

In the course of the dialogue the republican delegation too produced a set of proposals and suggested that both parties, Sinn Féin and the SDLP, could usefully consider the possibility of agreement on these:

1 That Sinn Féin and the SDLP agree with, and endorse, the internationally established principle of the right of the Irish people to national self-determination.

2 That Sinn Féin and the SDLP agree that Britain has no legitimate right to be in Ireland.

3 That Sinn Féin and the SDLP agree that the IRA is politically motivated in its actions and that IRA volunteers are not criminals. [In the talks Sinn Féin argued that armed struggle was about achieving political demands for national self-determination, an end to partition and the creation of a thirty-two-county Irish republic. Armed struggle, it said, was 'a political option' and was something that was 'forced upon the IRA'.]

4 That Sinn Féin and the SDLP agree that the British government and its forces in Ireland are not in a peacekeeping role.

5 That Sinn Féin and the SDLP would agree that failure to rule out nationalist participation in a devolved or internal six-county arrangement actually encourages the British to pursue such policies and in reality would protract the conflict.

6 That Sinn Féin and the SDLP agree on a common solution to the political situation existing in the six counties.

7 That Sinn Féin and the SDLP join forces to impress on the Dublin government the need to launch an international and diplomatic offensive to secure national self-determination.

In its response to these proposals, the SDLP restated its view that the Irish people had the right to self-determination but were divided on how that right should be exercised, and that it was the search for agreement that was the real challenge. Agreement on the right to self-determination would not be won by 'armed struggle', the SDLP said: while the IRA might be politically motivated, 'no legitimacy' could be conferred on its actions: 'To do so would concede the right of the majority of the Irish people to determine the means by which agreement in Ireland can be pursued to an unrepresentative and non-elected, non-accountable paramilitary organisation.' The party stated its view that all forms of violence were counterproductive and created barriers to achieving political progress. On the issue of future political structures, it said it had never argued for 'a purely internal settlement'. 'The SDLP has repeatedly made clear that relationships between Ireland and Britain as well as relationships within Ireland need to be resolved satisfactorily if there is to be lasting peace and stability.' The SDLP also said it would be prepared to enter into meaningful dialogue with any political party 'which receives a popular mandate and which uses democratic and peaceful methods, with a view to working for agreement in Ireland. To this end the SDLP would also join with such parties to seek such international support as would be appropriate.'

In the course of the 1988 talks, the SDLP also tried to persuade Sinn Féin that in the search for political agreement Britain had taken up a neutral position. John Hume and his colleagues used Article 1 of the 1985 Anglo-Irish Agreement to support their argument:

> In that Article, in the SDLP's view, the British government have made clear that if the people of the unionist and nationalist traditions in Ireland reach agreement on the unity and independence of Ireland, then the British government will legislate for it, facilitate it, and leave the people of Ireland, North and South, to govern themselves. In short, they are stating that Irish unity and independence are entirely a matter for those Irish people who want it, persuading those Irish people who don't. It is clear from Article 1 and the Preamble to the Agreement that the British government have no other interest at stake in the exercise of Irish self-determination except that violence or the threat of violence shall not succeed. In this context the 'armed struggle' can only be a negative factor.

But by the end of these delegation talks in September 1988, Sinn Féin had not been persuaded of British neutrality. Indeed Gerry Adams had this to say in his closing statement:

> This claim ignores all the historic evidence of British domination in Ireland and is wholly contradicted by the events of the past

twenty years, all of which point to the continuing commitment of the British government to impose its will by force on the Irish people through the maintenance of partition and continuing loyalist dominance of the six-county state. In the face of British government injustice and oppression the SDLP, to substantiate claims that the British are neutral, can only point to Article 1 of the Hillsborough Treaty [Anglo-Irish Agreement, 1985] despite the fact that the loyalist veto is explicitly contained within this Article, despite the fact that the British government asserts that the treaty is a 'bulwark against a united Ireland' and despite the fact that even Charles Haughey recognised the treaty to be a 'copper-fastening of partition'. To confer neutrality on the British government would be to confer neutrality on the Turkish government whose military invasion has partitioned the island of Cyprus. The Sinn Féin delegation, in attempting to explore the SDLP policy of 'unity by consent', was dismayed to discover that contained within this policy was a recognition and acceptance of the loyalist veto. The SDLP now appear to accept as absolute the power of veto of a national minority to obstruct and thwart the democratic right of the Irish people as a whole to exercise national self-determination. This position is of course untenable for a party which claims to act in the interests of Irish nationalists.

There were always going to be strains attached to these talks for as they continued so too did IRA violence. In the period of the discussions there were two bomb attacks – in Lisburn, County Antrim, and at Ballygawley, County Tyrone – which resulted in multiple deaths. In the two incidents fourteen soldiers were killed. There was also a series of IRA 'blunders' – attacks that led to the deaths of civilians – and before the delegation talks broke up in early September 1988 the IRA had reactivated its campaign in Britain by bombing an army barracks at Mill Hill in north London. Unionists were both deeply suspicious and fiercely critical of the talks, and some internal tension was also evident within the SDLP's own ranks. But, despite all this, John Hume believed that he and his party were involved in something that could prove worthwhile. In February 1995, with the IRA cessation by that stage into its sixth month, I discussed with the SDLP leader his analysis of the period leading to the ceasefire and I asked him when he had first become convinced that republicans were prepared to move away from 'armed struggle'. He 'sensed it' during those 1988 talks, he told me; his instinct was telling him they were serious.

But the 1988 round of talks ended not in the achievement of 'agreement on an overall nationalist political strategy for justice and peace' but with very real differences still separating both parties on the major issues of British neutrality, national self-determination and the unionist 'veto'. Nevertheless these talks were important, indeed it could be argued crucial, in terms of laying the foundations for a dialogue and a process that would eventually persuade republicans that the dynamic for an alternative 'unarmed strategy' had been created.

And as the talks between the SDLP leader and Gerry Adams moved into a phase of private and secret dialogue – something that would not be exposed until April 1993 – Hume was to become more and more convinced of the republicans' serious intent.

3

TRAVELLING A DIFFICULT ROAD

The road ahead was a difficult one; on the surface there was little sign of change – and there was still no sign of an end to the killing. In October 1988 the British government introduced broadcasting restrictions which by and large prevented the voice of Sinn Féin from being heard on radio and television, but the IRA was not silenced. In September 1989, the IRA bombed the Royal Marines School of Music at Deal in Kent; the explosion killed eleven bandsmen. During the Easter period in 1990, four soldiers in the Ulster Defence Regiment were killed by a landmine, and just three months later three police officers died in a similar attack when their vehicle was caught in a bomb trap as it travelled along a road in Armagh. A nun journeying along the same stretch of road was also killed in the explosion. Things were bad, but they got even worse as the year progressed, for 1990 also produced the so-called 'human bomb' attacks – incidents in which the IRA forced civilians to drive massive bombs to security posts. In the worst of these attacks, five soldiers were killed at a checkpoint in Derry. The sixth victim, Patsy Gillespie, a civilian employee at a security camp and therefore a 'collaborator' in the eyes of the IRA, had been forced to drive the bomb to its target and died in the blast. Even after twenty years of unbroken violence this was new and horrific; for many, this latest product of the IRA campaign was beyond belief. Despite the many expressions of revulsion, however, the killing kept happening. Indeed, just weeks after the horror of the human bombs, two police officers and two of their friends were found dead on the shores of Lough Neagh having been ambushed by the IRA while on a wildfowling trip. In the months and years ahead there would, tragically, be many more acts of violence involving the IRA and the loyalist groups.

In February 1991 an IRA attack in Britain made news headlines across the world. In the midst of the Gulf War and while Britain's War Cabinet was in session at the prime minister's residence in London's Downing Street, the IRA launched three mortar bombs at the building. No one was hurt, but the IRA's 'war' with Britain once again had won the attention of the world's media. In a statement afterwards, the IRA called on the British government to initiate a process that would lead to a British withdrawal from Northern Ireland. Both the demand and the language in which it was couched were familiar. At the time, Northern Ireland was just weeks away from yet another attempt to reach political accommodation through dialogue.

The following month, after a lengthy process of 'talks about talks', the secretary of state at the Northern Ireland Office, Peter Brooke, announced to the House of Commons that talks involving the four main constitutional parties in Northern Ireland – the Ulster Unionist Party, the Democratic Unionist Party, the Social Democratic and Labour Party and the Alliance Party – were to take place during a defined gap in Anglo-Irish Conference meetings. These talks would also involve the British and Irish governments and would be part of a three-strand process. This would look at future political structures for Northern Ireland and would also examine relationships between Northern Ireland and the Republic and between the British and Irish governments.

During the run-up to the talks I was asked to turn up at the headquarters of the then still legal Ulster Defence Association on 17 April 1991. At the building, on the Newtownards Road in east Belfast, I made my way through the security cage that enclosed the stairs and headed for a small room where four men were already seated at a round table. They were there to brief three reporters including myself: the occasion was to prove important because of the statement the men had been authorised to pass on. That statement was the first to be issued in the name of the Combined Loyalist Military Command, and its text read as follows:

> In the light of impending political dialogue and in common with a sincere and genuine desire to see a peaceful and acceptable solution to our political differences, the combined command of all loyalist military organisations shall order a universal suspension of aggressive operational hostilities commencing midnight of the night preceding the political summit. The timescale of such a suspension will be dependent upon the positive outcome of the respective stages through which the political exchanges may pass. Hinging on the principled flexibility of all the participating politicians, the forthcoming series of talks could prove, for the first time in our turbulent history, decisive in reaching an accommodation whereby all people of goodwill in Ulster, and further, irrespective of their calling, could claim that this is indeed a new beginning and should be given an opportunity to take root and flourish. Those in physical opposition to such an accommodation will rightly be seen to be against the democratically expressed wishes of the overwhelming majority of the people inhabiting our neighbouring islands and will be further isolated accordingly. The Combined Loyalist Command is cognisant that republican forces will probably attempt to disrupt this important and constructive political dialogue and to provoke a premature conclusion to the suspension of aggressive operational hostilities. So let them therefore be warned that the Combined Command will order defensive and, where fitting, retaliatory action if so required. Such action will be extremely discriminatory and to grave effect.

Reports of the impending loyalist ceasefire began to run at around teatime that evening, but within a matter of hours UFF gunmen had murdered a Catholic taxi driver, John O'Hara, in Belfast. The political talks were still twelve days away, and in the hiatus before they got underway the loyalist attacks continued. Indeed, as John O'Hara was being buried another taxi driver was shot and wounded in the city, this time by the UVF.

As for the IRA, it was dismissive of the CLMC ceasefire statement and expressed the view that neither that ceasefire nor the scheduled talks at Stormont could or would address 'the root cause of the conflict in Ireland' – that root cause according to the IRA being the denial of the Irish people's right to national self-determination. The IRA described the loyalist organisations as 'pro-British death squads' and said it reserved the right to take action against those who either organised or carried out attacks against members of the nationalist community:

> Should these death squads decide to become inactive, then the IRA will monitor the situation and act accordingly in regard to them. The British government and their forces bear ultimate respons-ibility for the conflict and our armed struggle is aimed primarily at them.

The loyalist terrorist leadership responded that the suspension of its violent campaign was a sincere attempt to bring about an at-mosphere that would give the political talks the best possible chance of success, and it accused the IRA of 'offering nothing'.

The talks themselves lasted a little over nine weeks but on 3 July 1991 Peter Brooke told Parliament that he had brought them to a conclusion. Though he said some progress had been made, those looking in from the outside could detect no sign of any movement towards a political settlement. The talks would later be reactivated by Brooke's successor at the Northern Ireland Office, Sir Patrick Mayhew, but then again there was no indication of the unionist and nationalist traditions being able to cut a deal.

The day after Brooke had made his statement to the Commons the predictable happened: the Combined Loyalist Military Com-mand announced that its ceasefire, begun at midnight on 29 April, would end at midnight on 4 July. In the nine or so weeks that it had been in place, loyalists had carried out two shootings. The UFF had murdered a Sinn Féin councillor, Eddie Fullerton, in his County Donegal home on 25 May and on 16 June the UVF had shot and wounded a man in north Belfast. On both occasions the respective loyalist groups said the shootings should not be read as an end to the ceasefire. The UFF argued that the terms of the ceasefire did not prevent it from carrying out attacks in the Irish Republic, and it said it would continue to carry out such attacks for so long as the Irish constitution continued to claim jurisdiction over Northern Ireland. As for the UVF, it said the shooting attack it carried out was a response to the high level of IRA activity at the time. This was the only act of loyalist violence in Northern Ireland during the ceasefire period – a period in which the IRA was particularly active and during which it was accused of trying to provoke a loyalist response.

In all there were thirteen IRA killings; among those who died were a prominent member of the Orange Order, a Protestant businessman and Cecil McKnight, a UDA member from Londonderry. This period of intense IRA activity also included a series of bombings, two of which happened in predominantly Protestant housing areas of Cookstown and Donaghcloney. At the time, republicans were dismissive of suggestions that much of this violence was overtly sectarian and designed to infuriate loyalists, but that was the clear impression held by the loyalists themselves. Indeed, when the CLMC ended its ceasefire it did so with these words:

> We have proven that we have a desire for peace, which can be seen as genuine, and have no vested interest in the continuation of violence. We have also demonstrated since the start of the talks that we are disciplined organisations. Proof has been our responsible reaction to the blatant sectarian attacks on Protestant/loyalist hous-ing estates, individuals and organisations carried out by republican murder gangs.

When I discussed this period with a loyalist paramilitary source some years later, he told me that loyalists had not expected such a surge of violence from the IRA: 'We certainly didn't expect them to be so blatantly sectarian.' Loyalists now believe that the IRA took a conscious policy decision to embark on a series of sectarian attacks.

In my research for this book I also spoke to David Ervine, a former loyalist prisoner who after serving a jail term for possession of explosives joined the fringe Progressive Unionist Party, which has links with the UVF. That was in 1984; ten years later he had emerged as one of the most prominent and capable spokesmen within loyalism. In early November 1994, in the upstairs lounge of a social club in the heart of Protestant east Belfast, we discussed a wide range of issues including the period leading to that 1991 loyalist ceasefire. Ervine told me that by the late 1980s there were those within loyalism who believed that republicans were beginning to fly 'peace kites'. He pointed to the Sinn Féin peace strategy and to the party's 1988 talks with the SDLP, and he said within loyalism there was a sense that perhaps the IRA had realised that it would have to settle for less than its stated aims. Within the loyalist camp there was a feeling of strength – 'even though there was a feeling of siege because of IRA violence and a feeling of betrayal because of the Anglo-Irish Agreement'. The Brooke talks, Ervine said, had provided loyalists with an opportunity to make a gesture. The talks were 'essentially the first time that the two great monoliths [unionism and nationalism] had got together in sixteen years', and this was significant given 'the violent tragedy of Northern Ireland'. Behind the scenes within loyalism it was being argued that loyalists must not be seen to be the barrier to peace. So the ceasefire was agreed. It crumbled, according to Ervine, not because of IRA provocation but as a result of the failure of the talks themselves.

When I spoke to Gerry Adams in March 1995 I discussed this period with him too, and in the course of our conversation the Sinn Féin president made reference to 'some quite good statements' by Peter Brooke. Brooke had held the position of secretary of state for Northern Ireland between July 1989 and April 1992 and in that time had spoken of Britain having no 'selfish, strategic or economic interest' in Northern Ireland; he had also said that it was difficult to envisage a military defeat of the IRA. But Gerry Adams expressed the view that those inter-party talks initiated by Brooke and followed through by his successor Sir

Patrick Mayhew were never going anywhere. For a start, Adams said, they were not 'inclusive' – in other words they excluded Sinn Féin. So, as 1991 came to a close, a political stalemate still prevailed. In the weeks after the loyalist ceasefire ended the UFF shot dead three Sinn Féin members including party councillor Bernard O'Hagan, while the IRA embarked on a bombing campaign aimed at 'economic targets'. These attacks left behind many surreal images of the conflict – of battered buildings and twisted wreckage not just in Belfast and provincial towns across Northern Ireland but also eventually in the very heart of the British capital.

4

SHOOTING AWAY THE BALLOT BOX

For more than a decade, the twin strategy of the republican movement had been encapsulated within the buzz phrase 'the Armalite
and the ballot box'. The phrase was first coined in 1981 by one of
the principal strategists of modern republicanism, Danny Morrison,
who spoke at that year's Sinn Féin ard-fheis (annual conference)
of republicans taking power 'with an Armalite in one hand and a
ballot paper in the other'. His comments were aimed primarily at
an internal republican audience at a time when Sinn Féin was
moving towards formal participation in electoral politics in
Northern Ireland, but outside that movement the words came to
be used to sum up the dual armed and political strands of
republican strategy.

Those two strands of policy were still very much in evidence as
1992 began to unfold. In January, eight Protestant men returning
from work at an army base in Omagh, County Tyrone, were killed
when their van was caught in an IRA bomb trap at Teebane Cross.
The Teebane bombing brought the inevitable loyalist response:
five Catholics were shot dead in Sean Graham's bookmaker's shop
on the Ormeau Road in Belfast on 5 February – a UFF statement
that followed this latest slaughter ended with the words 'remember
Teebane'. It was an all too predictable pattern of killing: reprisal
and then words of revenge. Just twenty-four hours before that
UFF attack on the Ormeau Road, three men had been shot dead
at the Republican Press Centre on Belfast's Falls Road – not by
loyalists but by an off-duty police officer who later killed himself.
In the middle of this mad month an extra battalion of troops was
deployed in Northern Ireland and before the month ended there

were more deaths. On 16 February the IRA carried out a gun attack on Coalisland RUC station and minutes later four of its members were shot dead by undercover soldiers. These were the heaviest IRA losses since those in Loughgall in May 1987 (eight IRA members killed), Gibraltar in March 1988 (three IRA members killed), Drumnakilly in August 1988 (three IRA members killed) and Coagh in June 1991 (three IRA members killed).

It was against this background that in mid-February Sinn Féin published a rewritten version of its peace strategy under the title *Towards a Lasting Peace*. The document offered an updated republican analysis of the conflict in Northern Ireland and set out the type of political action Sinn Féin believed to be necessary if the causes of that conflict were to be eradicated. The pamphlet said the achievement of peace would require a peace process focusing primarily on the right to national self-determination; in a section headed 'A Strategy for Change', republicans summed up their aims as follows:

> To secure maximum national and international political and popular support for the principles:
>
> – The recognition by the British government that the Irish people have the right to national self-determination;
>
> – That the British government change its current policy to one of ending partition and handing over sovereignty to an all-Ireland government whose selection would be a democratic matter for the Irish nation;
>
> – That the future of the unionists lies in this context and that the British government has a responsibility so to influence unionist attitudes;
>
> – That as part of this process the Dublin and London governments should consult together to seek agreement on the policy objective of ending partition.
>
> Having agreed this, both governments should issue a public statement outlining the steps they intend taking to bring about a peaceful and orderly British political and military withdrawal from Ireland within a specified period.

In all of this republicans were suggesting that the British government should actively attempt to persuade unionists towards Irish unity – a role that British governments have refused to undertake.

In its revised peace strategy Sinn Féin also outlined a proposed role for nationalist parties such as the SDLP in the North and Fianna Fáil in the South – parties recognised by Sinn Féin as having considerable political influence in Westminster, Washington and Brussels:

> These parties are in a position to harness the considerable sympathy for Irish reunification and sovereignty which exists in Europe and further afield. It is essential that they move decisively to implement their stated objectives and policies. If the six counties is regarded by the SDLP and the Dublin government as a non-viable context for a resolution of the conflict, let them firmly and explicitly reject partitionist scenarios.

This section of the document then went on to say: 'If the nationalist parties wish to believe that Britain has no selfish interest in remaining in Ireland, they should demand that Britain actually carries out that statement to its logical conclusion and formally accept the right of the Irish people to self-determination.' The clear republican objective was the creation of a pan-nationalist consensus to promote a political agenda set in an all-Ireland context. In other words, Sinn Féin wanted a peace process backed by significant nationalist political forces in Ireland and supported internationally by Irish-America.

On the sixteenth and final page of *Towards a Lasting Peace* eight points were set out in summary form:

1 Peace requires conditions of democracy, freedom and justice to eradicate the causes of war.
2 The Irish people have the same right to sovereignty and nationhood exercised throughout history and recognised in international law as any other nation. The partition of Ireland contravenes recognised international norms and frustrates national democracy and reconciliation in the country.

28

3 British rule in Ireland lacks democratic legitimacy either domestically or internationally and has rested predominantly on division and coercion. The British government should recognise the historical failure of the partition of Ireland in 1921.

4 The Dublin government should assume its responsibility to gain the reunification of the country, in co-operation with the British government or, if necessary, independently.

5 The unionist minority in Ireland has nothing to fear from a united Ireland. Withdrawal of the unionist veto will open the possibility of a constructive dialogue with the rest of the Irish people.

6 Irish republicans are determined to play a constructive role in building a national democracy in Ireland when a British government is convinced either by continuing armed resistance or by an effective unarmed constitutional strategy to adopt a policy of withdrawal from Ireland.

7 Ireland is a part of Europe which is undergoing an historic process of political and economic transformation. This will be incomplete while the Anglo-Irish conflict continues. The partition of Ireland and the British claim to jurisdiction over the six counties is a European issue. Sinn Féin seeks a democratic and sovereign Ireland which will defend the interests of all sections of the Irish nation.

8 The UN [United Nations] has the authority and mandate to monitor a decolonisation process in Ireland. As an interim measure Sinn Féin would propose that the UN Secretary-General requests annual reports from the British government on its role in Ireland and conducts a yearly review of the consequences of the continued partition of Ireland.

Interestingly, in the sixth of those eight summary points republicans pointed to their willingness to consider an effective unarmed strategy, a point that will be dealt with later. I want to focus here on the internal republican debate. *Towards a Lasting Peace* was the result of a Sinn Féin review of its peace strategy which had begun in February 1991 and entailed a close examination of *A Scenario for Peace*. In an article in the *Starry Plough* (issue no. 4), Mitchel McLaughlin, who is now his party's national chairman, provides the following insight into developments in republican thinking.

> Sinn Féin's analysis as presented in *Scenario for Peace* was seriously flawed because it did not deal adequately with the social and economic implications of a British withdrawal or with the constant changes and developments in international politics. This was a major political shortcoming which had to be addressed, not least because our opponents were exploiting the changes in Europe and the ending of the Cold War to project our arguments as old-fashioned and irrelevant. The ongoing review of republican strategy accepted that there were major credibility problems with other aspects of the *Scenario for Peace* arguments.

In his article McLaughlin, who is viewed as one of the key strategists within republicanism, said that in order for a document of the nature of *A Scenario for Peace* to be convincing, it should have included the following:

- A coherent statement on how a British withdrawal would be timetabled and accomplished.
- Detail concerning the consequences of a 'power vacuum'. Sinn Féin talks of British withdrawal and the disbandment of the RUC but what would fill the vacuum? Would the various strands of society in the North simply grab territory and build barricades?
- The republican movement's attitude on the possibility of a loyalist backlash, of how such a nightmare scenario could be avoided.
- Any viable peace project had to be supported by a detailed and viable economic analysis.

In summing up, Mitchel McLaughlin said the basic difference between the two documents was that *A Scenario for Peace* stated the case for a British withdrawal without reference to the political complexities, while *Towards a Lasting Peace* attempted to confront some of them. The primary objective for Sinn Féin at the end of this strategy review was to open up a debate around its aim of the magazine, the Sinn Féin president Gerry Adams said that all-inclusive talks were required to resolve the conflict and as part of this there needed to be a new agreement between London and Dublin to end partition. International assistance would also be required to help 'break the deadlock'.

In February 1995, I travelled to Armagh to speak to Cardinal Cahal Daly and to hear from him his thoughts on the process that had led the IRA to its August 1994 cessation of military operations. The cardinal has always been seen as a fierce critic of violence, both republican and loyalist, and both as a bishop based in Belfast and then as leader of Ireland's Catholics, he consistently refused any direct contact with Sinn Féin. What he did do, however, was to use many of his public addresses to engage republicans in debate, to try to persuade them to end violence and to choose instead the political, democratic path. In our conversation, Cardinal Daly touched on the 'contradictions' within the republican strategy – 'contradictions' attached to the continuation of the IRA's violent campaign while at the same time Sinn Féin was publishing its peace strategies. 'I would suppose that the people who framed those documents were disappointed that they weren't taken more seriously by the public at large, and I just wonder whether the reason why they were not being taken seriously and why their content wasn't being seriously studied was that they seemed to be contradicted by what they were doing on the ground in their whole armed struggle activities; because there was an obvious contradiction in the eyes of the public, the great majority of people in the general public, that to talk about peace on the one hand, to write about peace on the one hand, to have a scenario for peace and then to go on with destructive and life-taking activities was contradictory in itself.'

The cardinal believes that the real effect of the twin strategy operated by the republican movement was that the Armalite was shooting away the ballot box. He believes that republicans came to see that they could not build a strong, popular, electoral base while 'armed struggle' continued. He also sees the publication of the peace strategies as giving some indication of the nature of the debate that was going on within the ranks of republicanism. 'It seemed to me that successive documents reflected an intense debate which was going on on all aspects of the republican struggle. The armed strategy, the possibility of an unarmed strategy, the need for developing the socialist content of their thinking and to make it really a party of working-class struggle rather than of purely romantic republican aims, all these things were, I think, part of the ongoing debate which eventually culminated in the declaration of a ceasefire. So the ceasefire didn't seem to me to be coming out of a clear blue sky. It was gradually growing, a maturing development in republican thinking.'

Politically there was a setback for republicanism in the April 1992 Westminster elections: Gerry Adams, the sitting MP, lost in west Belfast to the SDLP's Joe Hendron, and on the night the Conservatives were returned to government an IRA bomb devastated part of London and caused three civilian deaths. The IRA said the bombing was 'a direct consequence of Britain's illegal occupation of Irish territory' and said similar attacks would be carried out for so long as Britain persisted in that occupation. So the two faces of republicanism were still very much in evidence. Sinn Féin won around 10 per cent of the poll in those Westminster elections, whilst the other strand of republican strategy, that of violent IRA activity, still plagued the political landscape.

It was in the period immediately following the Westminster elections that Sir Patrick Mayhew, a former Attorney-General, replaced Peter Brooke at the Northern Ireland Office. Soon afterwards another suspension of Anglo-Irish conference meetings was agreed to allow for a resumption of political talks. In the course of these, an Ulster Unionist delegation led by party leader James Molyneaux travelled to Dublin, but despite this historic journey there was no breakthrough and Northern Ireland remained trapped in violent conflict. The IRA bombed the commercial heart of Belfast on several occasions in 1992, and there were attacks in many provincial towns including Lurgan, Bangor and Coleraine.

The Belvoir housing estate in south Belfast was devastated when the IRA used a massive device to demolish the forensic science laboratory where evidence from the scenes of terrorist incidents was examined.

The violent loyalist groups were also particularly active during 1992, and their activity included attacks on Sinn Féin members. The north Belfast home of Gerard McGuigan, who at the time was the leader of the Sinn Féin elected representatives on Belfast City Council, was attacked in February; in a statement afterwards the UFF said it had 'the will and manpower to seek and destroy republicans'. There were no injuries in this incident but only weeks later, in April, a party election worker was shot dead at Kilrea in County Londonderry. Also in April, the UVF killed a member of the republican faction the Irish People's Liberation Organisation, the second figure within that group murdered by the UVF in Belfast since the 1991 loyalist ceasefire.

These attacks were all part of an upsurge in loyalist violence that began in the late 1980s and carried through into the 1990s. Part of the government response to this was to proscribe the UDA in August 1992, a move announced by Sir Patrick Mayhew at the Northern Ireland Office at Stormont Castle. Many believed this decision was long overdue: for many years those who had killed in the name of the Ulster Freedom Fighters had sheltered under the roof of the UDA. Just why the UDA was allowed to remain legal for so long is one of the great mysteries of the Northern Ireland conflict and something that has never been properly explained. Proscription, it has to be said, did nothing to curtail the terrorist activity being directed from within the UDA, but it did at least make illegal a paramilitary grouping that had been responsible for so much violence over such a long period of time.

Before the year was over loyalists shot dead another Sinn Féin member – this time a woman. Sheena Campbell was killed in a crowded Belfast bar in a gun attack described by the RUC as 'barbaric and ruthless'. The UVF said it had specifically targeted her and alleged she was an IRA activist, but Sinn Féin's Richard McAuley dismissed this and said that Sheena Campbell had been murdered because she had been prepared to stand up and articulate the views of her party. Gerry Adams highlighted what he called the 'demonisation' of his party and said this had created a climate in which it was seen as legitimate to kill members of Sinn Féin. He said Sheena Campbell was only one in a long line of nationalist women to be killed because of their political activity or because they happened to be Catholics.

The following month the UFF threatened to respond to recent IRA bombings, attacks which in many cases had happened in predominantly Protestant towns. In its statement the UFF warned that it would target the republican community 'as a whole'. A week later there was yet another indiscriminate gun attack on a bookmaker's shop. Within twenty-four hours of an IRA bomb attack in the centre of Coleraine, UFF gunmen fired shots into a betting shop on the Oldpark Road in north Belfast. Three Catholic men were killed – one of them a veteran of the Royal Air Force aged seventy-two.

The attack happened on Saturday 14 November 1992. That evening at around half past six I took a statement from the UFF in which it admitted the killings and threatened more of the same:

> The UFF warned last week what we would do if PIRA continued their sectarian attacks. Today we acted accordingly. We again warn Sinn Féin and PIRA that the theatre of war will be full of casualties from the republican community in the coming weeks.

In a follow-up news report I quoted a senior police source who spoke of the loyalist group 'satisfying a bloodlust'. He said the ordinary Protestant people were looking on in 'total disbelief'. As for republicans, Sinn Féin's Joe Austin said the UFF statement was an attempt to cover up for its actions: 'The UFF cannot hide behind the excuse that their actions are reactionary to those of others. The beleaguered north Belfast nationalist community has been burying the victims of loyalist terror for generations. Terror attacks by loyalists are an attempt to force nationalists into accepting loyalist domination and British control. That is why the British government's response to the actions of loyalist murder gangs is so muted.'

As the year ended, the UFF again tried to murder Catholics in a bookmaker's shop, once more in north Belfast, but in this incident a gun jammed and lives were spared. That night, 31 December 1992, the loyalist group issued one of its most threatening statements yet, warning what it called the 'pan-nationalist front' of the SDLP, the Irish government and the IRA of its bloody plans for the year ahead. The UFF boasted that it was 'fully armed and equipped' to intensify its campaign in 1993 'to a ferocity never imagined'. The loyalist group was now threatening to target the SDLP, the main constitutional nationalist party in Northern Ireland.

5

TAKING RISKS FOR PEACE

On a miserable night with the winter elements at play outside, I sat in a small office at the Markethill home of the SDLP deputy leader, Seamus Mallon MP. It was the first Sunday of the new year, 3 January 1993, and I was there to interview him about that threatened escalation of loyalist violence and more specifically the threat now hanging over his party. Mallon was treating the matter seriously, and indeed in the course of the interview he offered to meet face to face those who had issued the statement. He said the UFF knew that the members of his party, right across the north of Ireland, had stood up to the IRA in a way that probably nobody else had – this was something he would tell the UFF if it agreed to talk: 'I will go and talk to these people who make this threat. Are they man enough to sit across a table from me, and look me in the eyes, and to make that threat to me across the table, because I'm saying to you now, and saying to them, I will go anywhere they specify, I will talk to them, I will tell them what they are do-ing, I'll tell them the damage they are doing just the same as I have told other paramilitary groupings. I wonder have they the courage to take up that offer.'

As I journeyed back to Belfast on that dark winter's night, news began to break of yet another loyalist shooting, this one in County Tyrone where a father and his son had been murdered by the UVF. By teatime the following evening the UFF had rejected Seamus Mallon's offer. The terrorist group accused his party of blocking progress towards an accountable government in Northern Ireland and the MP responded by saying it was now clear that the UFF's courage came from behind masks.

The period ahead would bring more violence; the month of October would be the most violent in the recent history of the Northern Ireland Troubles and Northern Ireland would once more be pushed towards the edge, but slowly, painfully, things were moving in a different direction. The first attack on the SDLP took place in February: blast incendiary devices were left outside the homes of two city councillors in Belfast. The incidents happened on the eve of an Anglo-Irish intergovernmental conference meeting (a meeting of British and Irish ministers) – a gathering described by the UFF as 'undemocratic and corrupt'. In the months ahead there was a spate of similar incidents at the homes of SDLP members, attacks that intensified in the latter part of 1993 following the disclosure of secret talks between John Hume and Gerry Adams. Some of those targeted were prominent party figures such as the west Belfast MP Dr Joe Hendron and the former city councillor and Stormont Assembly member Brian Feeney, whilst others were less well known. After one series of incidents the secretary of state, Sir Patrick Mayhew, spoke of an 'overt attack on democracy'. In two of the attacks on the SDLP the UFF subsequently said its intention had been to kill. The violent assault on republicanism also continued. Sinn Féin party members Peter Gallagher and Alan Lundy were shot dead in Belfast – the latter at the Andersonstown home of party councillor Alex Maskey, who had been the intended target of the UFF shooting – and IRA member James Kelly was killed along with three other men when their van was ambushed by the UFF at Castlerock, County Londonderry. There were attacks too on the homes of Sinn Féin members Gerard McGuigan, Joe Austin, Annie Armstrong and Bobby Lavery. In the latter incident one of Councillor Lavery's sons was killed. Afterwards a senior loyalist said to me that the shooting would 'hurt him and them', a reference both to Bobby Lavery and Sinn Féin. In this spate of attacks, too, a grenade was thrown at the family home of the Sinn Féin president Gerry Adams. One Shankill loyalist later boasted that the UFF, in its targeting of Sinn Féin, had attacked 'the top, middle and bottom of the ladder'.

There was no sign of any let-up in IRA violence either. In March 1993, I travelled to Derry to interview one of the most influential figures within republicanism, Martin McGuinness. The purpose of the interview was to draw from him his assessment of the political and security situation at that time – an assessment I knew would be useful in determining the mood throughout the republican movement. What I did not know at the time of this interview was that by now, McGuinness was already involved in secret contacts between the British government and the republican leadership – contacts that would not be exposed until the following November. At our meeting McGuinness told me that in the search for a settlement to the conflict there would be no unilateral IRA move: a formula would have to be found in which the British government and 'republican forces' moved at the same time. Even if talks were to take place there would be no guarantee that they would bring an end to armed conflict: 'The British government, in the past, have been asked by us to involve themselves in talks. To be quite honest I find it boringly repetitious to be saying again that talks should take place. I'm not going to say that, but I believe that an opportunity does exist and that instead of the British government stating categorically that the IRA must move unilaterally, I think that they must be more open-minded about it. They must show courage and they must accept that that is not going to happen and that both sides must move together, that both sides must take the first step.' What was lacking, McGuinness said, was a willingness on the part of the British government to become involved in talks.

I then asked him whether, if talks were to take place, violence would end: 'There is no guarantee whatsoever that talks between republican forces or even Sinn Féin and the British government will bring an end to armed struggle. What is needed on behalf of the British government is a recognition that things are never going to be the same again and that there is going to have to be a different relationship between the British government and this island. McGuinness said he believed the republican goal of a united

Ireland was 'very much achieveable' and he suggested that there were many people within the unionist community who believed that the British government was going to 'sell them out', that the British government was going to leave. He did not believe that the situation was hopeless, but he said there was no doubt that we had 'a very dangerous situation'. 'What I see is a very determined IRA who appear to be very committed to prosecuting this struggle to its final conclusion. I think that the British government also recognise that that is a reality and I believe that makes it incumbent upon all sides to attempt to engage in the search for a peace process which will bring all this to an end.'

The McGuinness interview prompted responses from several different quarters. The DUP leader Ian Paisley once again said that the IRA must be militarily defeated; he said McGuinness had let the cat out of the bag by saying that Sinn Féin involvement in some future talks process would not guarantee an end to violence. The secretary of state, Sir Patrick Mayhew, re-emphasised his government's line that it would not sit down to talk with those who supported violence and who refused to denounce it. Meanwhile the SDLP deputy leader, Seamus Mallon, suggested some means of confidential dialogue to explore whether there was any potential for a breakthrough.

Certainly nothing was said by Martin McGuinness to suggest that the IRA might be preparing to step back from its campaign. Indeed, just a matter of days after that interview, the news was dominated by yet another violent incident, which caused the deaths of two young boys, Timothy Parry and Jonathan Ball. They were caught in two explosions in Warrington town centre on the Saturday before Mother's Day, and in the period immediately after this Gordon Wilson, whose daughter Marie had died in the Enniskillen bombing, asked to meet the IRA.

Gordon Wilson is not prepared to say where that meeting happened other than that it took place 'somewhere in Ireland'. In the years following the death of his daughter, Wilson had repeatedly asked himself if there was anything he could do to bring the situation in Northern Ireland 'a little nearer to peace'. During our conversation in Dublin on 2 February 1995 he told me that one answer, the only answer, that kept coming back to him was: 'Why don't you go and talk to the IRA, not to Sinn Féin.' Wilson used the media to make it known that he wanted such a meeting; he was subsequently told that the IRA would be in touch: 'I was going to talk to them fundamentally as Marie Wilson's father. I was not going, and I made it very clear, to negotiate, to mediate, to represent any party or group. I was representing Marie Wilson, but, this is important, I was also very publicly acknowledging that they too had had their losses.' Gordon Wilson knew he would be criticised and that some would say, 'How dare he'. But this was something he had to do to give himself some personal peace of mind.

On 6 April 1993, the night before the meeting, Gordon Wilson took a call in his room in a Dublin hotel. The gist of the message, he later told me, was that he should be in 'such and such a place' at two o'clock the following day. He would be met in a car park, and he was not to drive his own vehicle. He then telephoned his wife and told her that tomorrow would be 'a long day'. Joan Wilson understood the message and wished her husband well. A man whose daughter had died at the hands of the IRA was now just hours away from a meeting with senior representatives of that organisation. The journey was not a straightforward one but one involving a circuitous route as the IRA took precautions to ensure that its 'security' was not compromised.

'We went across fields and main roads and through farm gates and through three other private houses with a change of driver every time. It was bizarre.' One of the IRA representatives was a young woman. 'I would suggest in her late twenties. I would be pretty sure she was a graduate.' Gordon Wilson said the presence of this young woman in an IRA setting was depressing because for him it brought into focus the reality of 'second-generation terrorism'. The second IRA representative was a man. 'They told me what their names were. Frankly I've forgotten, but we'll say John and Mary. That's what I called them and they called me

Mr Wilson, and it was courteous.' The man, who kept his cap on, wore glasses: 'He, I'm bound to say, was a hard man. He answered the yes–no questions, but the shades of grey were covered by the girl. She was articulate and she had a mind . . . and a thinking mind.' In the lead-up to this meeting, Gordon Wilson had asked through one of his intermediaries if the IRA intended to record the conversation. If they did, he would do likewise. But he was told there would be no recording. He was therefore a little taken aback when a man with a notepad and pencil joined them in the room. In reply to a question from Gordon Wilson, the man explained that he was with the IRA and that he was there to take notes. Wilson insisted that he too should be given a copy. This was agreed, and he received a written summary of the meeting several weeks later. Gordon Wilson told me that he could not believe how remarkably 'cool and calm' he had been. He had expected to be nervous almost to the point of shaking, but the atmosphere was relaxed. 'We were drinking orange juice and coffee and eating buns and I couldn't believe how cool I was. I really couldn't.'

Gordon Wilson put it to the IRA that there had to be a better way for them to achieve their aim – a way other than 'terrorism and murder and the bomb and the bullet'. He said the IRA representatives produced two sheets of typed notes that had been wrapped in toilet paper – a measure to avoid the risk of leaving fingerprints. By the time Wilson had finished reading them he knew he was getting nowhere. He said what was being 'trotted out' was the stuff he had heard many times before and in his mind it boiled down to two words: 'Brits out'. He said he asked the IRA representatives if 'Brits out' meant Protestants out and he was told no, that the IRA's war was not with Protestants but with 'the forces of the Crown'. Gordon Wilson then asked those in the room to explain the Warrington bombing: 'I don't pretend to have much in the way of brain power but it was quite illogical. I couldn't understand how on the one hand they were telling me that they were fighting the British army and the forces of the Crown and yet they were killing two little boys in Warrington.'

41

The IRA representatives were holding to their statement and Gordon Wilson knew he was not making progress: 'I was under no illusion and I'm not foolish enough, I hope, to think that just because Gordon Wilson asked them to stop they were going to say, all right, Gordon, we've heard you, we're going to stop. I did, however, expect something, another word, a change of emphasis, a nuance even, something. I got nothing, not an inch in reverse but my conscience was clear. I had tried.' In the hours after the meeting, the IRA issued a statement to the media; Gordon Wilson held a news conference in Belfast the following day. Two years later he summed up his feelings by saying he had been 'up against a brick wall' and his mission was 'unaccomplished'. But although he failed, he has slept better since.

The day after Gordon Wilson's news conference, on Friday 9 April 1993 at a location in west Belfast a package was dropped onto a table in a small coffee shop where I was sitting alone. The man who dropped it muttered a few words and walked on. The package contained a propaganda video and under the image of masked and armed men roaming the countryside the IRA delivered its Easter message, the words of which were read by a woman: 'As we face into our twenty-fifth year of unbound and unbroken resistance we proclaim our determination not to desist from our efforts until our nation's sovereign right to self-determination is finally recognised. We call on our enemy to pursue the pathway to peace or resign themselves to the inevitability of war.'

6

SHATTERING ILLUSIONS

It was against the backdrop of Warrington, Gordon Wilson's meeting with the IRA and that Easter video message that the secret dialogue then taking place between the SDLP leader John Hume and the Sinn Féin president Gerry Adams became public knowledge over the weekend of 10–11 April 1993. All this no doubt had something to do with the vitriolic and hostile reaction that was manifest in certain sections of the media. But there is no question that what John Hume and Gerry Adams were engaged in eventually created the conditions that brought about the IRA ceasefire announcement of 31 August 1994. Certainly that is John Hume's belief, and his analysis is endorsed by the Sinn Féin president. Cardinal Daly also recognises the important roles that both men had in the process of searching for a breakthrough. When, after the ceasefire, I spoke to him in Armagh he described Adams's role as 'absolutely crucial' and he said due credit should be paid 'to the courage, the commitment and the tenacity with which he patiently worked away at persuading the whole republican movement of the validity of the case he was putting forward – the democratic way forward'. The cardinal believes that John Hume's involvement in trying to persuade republicans to end 'armed struggle' came from 'his own deepest conviction about the wrongfulness of violence, the futility of violence and the need for dialogue and for agreement before there could be a peaceful settlement'. Cardinal Daly spoke too of 'very considerable movement' within republican thinking to the point that republicans realised 'that democratic dialogue is the only way towards justice and towards peace'.

The revelation of the Hume–Adams dialogue happened altogether by chance: the Sinn Féin president was seen visiting the home of the SDLP leader in Derry on Saturday 10 April, and the story ran the following day in the *Sunday Tribune*. The two men had been meeting privately over a 'long period' and Gerry Adams later told me they had reached consensus about the principles required for a peace settlement; he said their talks were probably the most significant element of the peace process in that they 'shattered the illusion' that the Northern conflict was intractable. Adams said that whilst others had surrendered to the notion that the conflict would go on forever, he and John Hume had demonstrated that there was an alternative.

Adams does not attempt to play down the importance of Hume's contribution to what he calls the 'peace process'; indeed, he believes that the SDLP leader played a vital part in reversing a political trend which the Sinn Féin president says was designed by the British government to ostracise his party and to put it beyond the pale. Adams here cites censorship and the British government's refusal to recognise Sinn Féin's electoral mandate. But, he says, John Hume broke that trend and then in the face of political and media vilification showed his 'mettle'. John Hume admits that in the course of this process he went through the worst period of his life, but in describing this time to me he spoke in terms of seeing the road ahead, of seeing the goal, and of refusing to be distracted by the shadows. He told me he knew he would be 'crucified' if he failed but that this didn't matter: if he had just been playing politics, he told me, he would have chucked it, but he had recognised there was a real opportunity to save human lives.

In compiling the research for this book, after weeks of trying I finally got to sit across a table from the SDLP leader on 27 February 1995, by which time the IRA ceasefire was close to six months old. Hume drank black coffee, smoked continuously and talked almost in a whisper. He was restless, fidgeting with his lighter, and he struck me as a man still under immense pressure – a man living a political life which demanded of him that he rush from one appointment to the next. In all of this there was little or no time, it seemed, for relaxation. As we chatted he outlined the reasons for his dialogue with Gerry Adams. He spoke of his personal belief that republicans were prepared to move away from their armed campaign. The conversation focused on the tensions and emotions attached to that long and dangerous search for a breakthrough, and John Hume said he had felt that if anyone could deliver a cessation of republican violence it was the president of Sinn Féin.

John Hume believes that his dialogue with Gerry Adams, out of which a still secret 'Hume–Adams agreement' emerged, was 'totally central' to the arrival at the ceasefire on 31 August 1994. The SDLP leader said he had acknowledged from the outset of the contacts, going back to 1988, that he was dealing with people 'who actually believed in what they were doing'. In his mind they could not be dismissed as gangsters or criminals: 'It was because they actually believed in what they were doing that they were the force they were and I, as a trained Irish historian, recognised that they were a direct product of history and that the philosophy that they were pursuing was a traditional Irish republican philosophy.'

At the time of his debate with republicans, John Hume made public in some detail the statistics of death – figures that he said showed that the IRA had killed six times more people than the British army, the RUC and the UDR put together. He asked how such acts of violence could be justified. The other central aspect of the debate focused on the stated reasons for what republicans called 'armed struggle': 'The major debate between us took place on their traditional reasons. It was on the whole question of self-determination and on the question of the reasons for the British presence, and, basically, that's what the dialogue was about. My position was that the Irish people had the right [to self-determination] but unfortunately were divided on how the right was to be exercised; it was the search for agreement that was the real search for a solution, and the best way to do that peacefully was for all resources to be devoted to promoting agreement, particularly both governments'.'

John Hume also spoke to me of the importance of the speech by Peter Brooke at Whitbread in November 1990 (a speech also referred to by Adams – see page 24), in which he stated that Britain had no 'selfish, strategic or economic' interest in Northern Ireland. Hume believes those comments strengthened his argument that the traditional reasons for what the IRA called 'armed struggle' no longer existed. He also believes that the former taoiseach (Irish prime minister) Charles Haughey played a 'major role' in the efforts to bring about peace: 'When my dialogue with Gerry Adams started, Charlie Haughey was the taoiseach. I consulted him regularly and all my drafts were done in total consultation with him. And he was extremely encouraging and, in my opinion, played a major role in the whole development and when Albert Reynolds became taoiseach the matter was already very well in hand.' The SDLP leader said Reynolds was also 'very positive' and put the search for a peaceful settlement in the North at the top of his political agenda.

It was about a month after I had spoken to John Hume that I met Gerry Adams in a small office in a bookshop in west Belfast. A woman left a pot of tea brewing for us on top of a gas heater, and as we chatted the Sinn Féin president poured. This was a relaxed conversation and it was on the record. Gerry Adams had just updated his book, *Pathway to Peace*, and much of what I wanted to chat about was fresh in his mind. There were a hundred questions I wanted to ask, but time, or more precisely a lack of it, meant that not all of them would be put or dealt with. Richard McAuley, a close friend, confidant and press aide to Adams, stood in the corner of the room for the duration of the conversation. In the weeks and months that had just passed he had been at the shoulder of his party leader – McAuley is one of a group of republicans including Adams, Martin McGuinness, Jim Gibney, Mitchel McLaughlin, Tom Hartley, Pat Doherty, Rita O'Hare, Lucilita Breathnach, Siobhán O'Hanlon, Gerry Kelly, and Mairead Keane with a very clear understanding of the inner workings of what has become known as the Irish Peace Initiative. There are others of course, not known on the public stage, who have also been crucial to this whole process – a process that remains very sensitive and for that very reason republicans had taken a decision not to assist book projects like mine. It had therefore taken many phone calls to McAuley and a personal letter to Adams before the Sinn Féin president agreed to see me. In our conversation on Monday 27 March 1995, Adams told me that the agreement reached between himself and Hume in the talks that there could be no internal settlement in Northern Ireland had sent a clear message to the British and Irish governments and to the unionists that it was time for political change.

Hume and Adams issued the first joint public statement to come out of their talks following a meeting on 23 April 1993. It read as follows:

A meeting between us held on Saturday 10 April in our capacities as party leaders of the SDLP and Sinn Féin has given rise to media coverage, some of which was ill-informed or purely speculative. We are not acting as intermediaries. As leaders of our respective parties, we accept that the most pressing issue facing the people of Ireland and Britain today is the question of lasting peace and how it can best be achieved. Everyone has a solemn duty to change the political climate away from conflict and towards a process of national reconciliation, which sees the peaceful accommodation of the differences between the people of Britain and Ireland and the Irish people themselves. In striving for that end, we accept that an internal settlement is not a solution because it obviously does not deal with all the relationships at the heart of the problem. We accept that the Irish people as a whole have a right to national self-determination. This is a view shared by a majority of the people of this island, though not by all its people. The exercise of self-determination is a matter for agreement between the people of Ireland. It is the search for that agreement and the means of achieving it on which we will be concentrating. We are mindful that not all the people of Ireland share that view or agree on how to give meaningful expression to it. Indeed we cannot disguise the different views held by our own parties. As leaders of our respective parties, we have told each other that we see the task of reaching agreement on a peaceful and democratic accord for all on this island as our primary challenge. We both recognise that such a new agreement is only achieveable and viable if it can earn and enjoy the allegiance of the different traditions on this island, by accommodating diversity and providing for national reconciliation. We are reporting our discussion of these matters back to our respective parties. They have fully endorsed the continuation of this process of dialogue. We will be picking up on where the talks between our parties ended in 1988 and reviewing the current political situation. At that time, we engaged in a political dialogue aimed at investigating the possibility of developing an overall political strategy to establish justice and peace in Ireland.

The reality is that that process of picking up where the SDLP and Sinn Féin had left off in 1988 had begun much, much earlier. The fact that the dialogue had remained secret had convinced John Hume that it was worthwhile and that republicans were engaged in a serious exercise of exploring an alternative strategy. 'Throughout my dialogue I realised that Gerry Adams was totally straight with me in what he was saying to me and I think he accepted that I was totally straight with him. In other words, in spite of our deep differences a great deal of personal trust in our respective points of view built up. Throughout the dialogue I kept both governments fully informed, and that was the reason why Peter Brooke made his speech in November 1990. That shows you how long the dialogue was going on and that [the Brooke speech] was about the question of neutrality.'

Adams's views on the Brooke speech, it must be said, are significantly different. Despite his reference to 'some quite good statements' by Brooke when I spoke to him in March 1995, Gerry Adams still had not been persuaded of British neutrality on the question of a united Ireland. Adams said he believed that the British Establishment wanted a settlement but it was not a monolith: while he was certain there were elements within it that wanted to end the Union, there were others who wanted to maintain it: 'My one-sentence description of the British Establishment position is that they have no bottom line. They can be moved as far as the political influence or power that can be harnessed for a democratic solution; they will move as far as that can push them.'

In terms of that April 1993 Hume–Adams statement, the Sinn Féin president believes the most significant of the statements of principle was that relating to no internal solution. He said it sent a very clear signal that the political parties that represented nationalists in the North were not going back to past political structures at Stormont – that there had to be, in his view, a settlement outside of a partitionist arrangement. Adams also points to a wider significance attached to the process:

'I really think that the very important element of it, from a republican perspective, was that we [Sinn Féin] decided to engage our opponents on the whole issue of peace. So from our point of view that engagement met with the type of results of John Hume and me coming to agreement and then getting Dublin on board and then getting Irish-America on board. So what did John Hume and I do? After twenty-five years of conflict we shattered the illusion that this was intractable. Now, whether people do or do not subscribe to our notion of how it can actually be resolved is unimportant. The fact is that we said, this can be resolved, and then we proceeded and have proceeded since to try and bring about that resolution. It cannot be resolved until London fully engages in the process and even yet [March 1995] London have not fully engaged in the process and we cannot have a peace settlement unless unionists are persuaded to be part of it.' This last point again reflects the republican desire for Britain to be a persuader in relation to Irish unity – an invitation, as I mentioned earlier, that the government has declined to accept.

The first Hume–Adams statement was issued on 24 April 1993. The day before, in a speech in Liverpool, the secretary of state, Sir Patrick Mayhew, had spoken of the desire within the community for a resumption of political talks. He said he agreed with the prime minister, John Major, that 'much more success' had been achieved in the process than was publicly perceived and he gave a sketch of what his government believed was viable. A lasting settlement could only be achieved by dialogue between political representatives and the government was 'quite sure' that the talks process retained 'the potential to deliver a fair and widely acceptable accommodation'. The government had no blueprint but was preparing 'some propositions of a realistic and practical kind, which we hope will help focus discussion in any new talks'. The constitutional position of Northern Ireland as part of the United Kingdom was not going to change, 'save with the consent of a majority of the people of Northern Ireland, clearly expressed'. There would be no joint London–Dublin authority exercised in Northern Ireland, 'because as I read it, such an outcome would be quite unacceptable to public opinion there'. In his speech, Sir Patrick raised the possibility of a Northern Ireland select committee at Westminster, a cross-party parliamentary committee with authority to examine Northern Ireland affairs and then report its findings. (In December 1993 the prime minister announced a decision to create such a committee.)

Any hope, however, of a resumption of talks involving unionists disappeared with that Hume–Adams statement. Unionists were furious and made clear there would be no dialogue with the SDLP while its leader was talking with the Sinn Féin president. Things were looking pretty bad. Loyalists reacted violently and intensified their attacks on SDLP and Sinn Féin members. In April, a huge IRA bomb at Bishopsgate devastated part of London, and during the spring and summer the IRA embarked on another bombing campaign across Northern Ireland which left its mark on central Belfast, Portadown, Magherafelt and Newtownards. The Belfast bombing came at the time of local government elections in which Sinn Féin achieved a 12.4 per cent share of the poll, receiving just over 78,000 first-preference votes.

The second joint Hume–Adams statement was issued on 25 September 1993. In it the two party leaders said considerable progress had been made during their discussions and that a report on the position reached to date was to be sent to the Dublin government. In this statement the two men said they recognised that the broad principles of agreement emerging from their talks would be for wider consideration by the two governments, but it is difficult to judge the real importance of the statement, for in my conversations with John Hume and Gerry Adams I was told that both the British and Irish governments were aware of their broad principles of agreement as early as June 1993. When I spoke to Gerry Adams in March 1995 he told me that 'Hume–Adams' was still 'quite sensitive' but that it had 'quite quickly' become 'Hume–Adams–Dublin' and this is why republicans in particular have tended to refer to the process as the Irish Peace Initiative. Republicans also point to their published record of secret contacts with the British government (see Chapter 7) and specifically to a development dated 14 June 1993:

> The British government representative forwarded a text designated 'secret' to Sinn Féin. The secret text shows conclusively that the British government was fully aware of the detail of the Irish Peace Initiative at this point. This secret text is withheld because of its sensitivity.

The weeks that followed that Hume–Adams September statement were filled with political uncertainty and with horrific violence. Loyalists spoke of betrayal and of preparation for war, and all of this created a sense of fear not felt here since the very worst days of the Troubles back in the early seventies.

On Monday 27 September 1993, in response to the Hume–Adams statement, the UDA issued a statement saying it was the duty of the unionist/loyalist leadership to bring its people to a state of readiness 'in defence of their religious and political beliefs' in the face of what the paramilitary leadership described as this 'final act of betrayal'. The Inner Council of the UDA said the Hume–Adams statement had confirmed its long-held belief that there existed a 'joint agreed policy' between the leaders of the SDLP and Sinn Féin and had 'vindicated' its view that a pan-nationalist front existed. The statement from the UDA also called on the unionist leadership to prepare for a total withdrawal from all institutions of government. These, the paramilitary group said, were coming increasingly under the control of the pan-nationalist front. The general secretary of the Ulster Unionist Party, Jim Wilson, responded to that statement by saying that he could not think of a more inappropriate time for leaders of the unionist community to withdraw from elected office: 'Following the weekend's premature disclosure of the SDLP–Sinn Féin–Dublin linkage and faced with the proof, if indeed proof was needed, that there is a pan-nationalist front, the unionist leadership has to redouble its effort to represent the will of the vast majority of decent law-abiding citizens at all levels of the political process.'

On 6 October the UFF carried out a gun attack on the Derby House bar on the outskirts of west Belfast. One man was killed in the shooting, but the publicly stated intention of the loyalist group had been to inflict 'heavy casualties'. In a statement the UFF said that attacks on the nationalist community would intensify 'while their representatives in the pan-nationalist front negotiate over the heads of the loyalist people'. The statement also posed the question: 'What price peace, Mr Hume?' Virtually every day that followed brought news of yet more violence. There were gun attacks on taxis travelling into nationalist areas of Belfast, and after one of these incidents the UFF said its aim had been to cause 'mass murder'. On 12 October in east Belfast the UVF ambushed a van carrying Catholic workers. One man died and several others were wounded. Three days later another man, Patrick McMahon, was shot dead by the UFF in north Belfast. In a statement issued after the incident the loyalist organisation spoke of 'assassinating' a 'nationalist'. Gone was the pretence of targeting republican activists: there was a general feeling at this time that the UFF had declared war on the entire Catholic community.

This pattern of violence continued and, indeed, led to something much, much worse. On 23 October 1993 the IRA carried out a bomb attack on the Shankill Road, in the heart of Protestant Belfast. A device containing Semtex high explosive was carried into a fish shop and exploded within seconds. Under the rubble of the collapsed building nine innocent civilians including women and children lay dead alongside one of the IRA bombers, Thomas Begley. The intention of the IRA had been to target an office above the fish shop – an office that had been the official headquarters of the UDA in west Belfast before its proscription and which was still used as a regular meeting place by prominent Shankill loyalists including one man in particular whom the IRA had actively been targeting. But the office was empty at the time of the explosion. In the days leading up to the Shankill bombing the IRA had warned that there would be no hiding place for those involved with what it called the 'loyalist death squads': 'We are determined to exact a price from them. No one should be under any illusions. Those involved with the loyalist death squads will be held accountable for their actions.' However, in the aftermath of the Shankill explosion, which destroyed so many families, it was Sinn Féin who was being asked to explain and account for the actions of the IRA, particularly with so much talk of peace at that time.

After I left the scene of the explosion and returned to the office a statement from the UFF was telephoned to the BBC newsdesk by an anonymous caller – a statement that contained a predictable and chilling threat. It said the loyalist people of west Belfast had been on the receiving end of 'a blatantly indiscriminate bomb attack supposedly aimed at the leadership of the UFF', and then went on to say: 'As from 18.00 hours tonight all Brigade area active service units of the UFF across Ulster will be fully mobilised. John Hume, Gerry Adams and the nationalist electorate will pay a heavy, heavy price for today's atrocity.' That heavy price would mean thirteen more deaths in the seven days that lay ahead – killings which would involve both the UFF and the UVF.

Those incidents included an attack on a council yard in west Belfast on 26 October in which two men were shot dead and five others were wounded by the UFF. Two days later, the UVF murdered two young brothers at their isolated home at Bleary in County Down and on Saturday 30 October the UFF carried out an attack on the Rising Sun pub in Greysteel in County Londonderry. Seven people were killed and an eighth died later. In a brutally cold sense the UFF had achieved its objective. In that surge of violence it had matched the Shankill body count. These were horrific times: days when lives and dreams were shattered in a bloody period of mad killing, days when hope was nowhere to be found, days as a journalist I had never experienced before. And I don't mind admitting there were times when I felt like walking away. John Hume told me that emotionally this period almost finished him, but he drew strength from conversations that he had with relatives of Shankill and Greysteel victims who told him to keep going. In keeping going the SDLP leader was putting himself at risk. In various loyalist statements he and Gerry Adams were referred to as the 'joint chiefs of staff' of pan-nationalism and there is no question that as he worked to persuade republicans to end violence the SDLP leader's life was on the line. The UFF was 'actively targeting' him on both sides of the border – this was something I had confirmed by both loyalist and security sources during my research for this book.

In the period immediately after the Shankill bombing the Dublin government appeared to distance itself from the Hume–Adams initiative. That cooling process became evident when the Irish foreign minister and Labour Party leader, Dick Spring, first outlined his own set of principles designed to give political direction to the search for a peaceful settlement in the North. In these he underscored the need for consent before there could be any constitutional change in Northern Ireland. He pointed out that those who were engaged in violence could only come to the negotiating table if the killing ended. This intervention by Spring, who had played a key role in the negotiations leading to the Anglo-Irish Agreement in 1985, was made on 27 October, the day after Gerry

Adams had carried the coffin of the Shankill bomber, Thomas Begley. This was a sight that offended many, but those who know Adams and who know the mind of the man hardly blinked an eyelid. As I mentioned in the preface to this book, Gerry Adams is the father of modern-day republicanism and while he has on occasions criticised IRA actions that have resulted in civilian deaths, he has never condemned that organisation and nor has he washed his hands of it.

Another significant development occurred on 29 October when in Brussels the British and Irish prime ministers, John Major and Albert Reynolds, issued a joint statement taking on board much of what had been said two days earlier by Dick Spring. The need for the support of a majority of people living in Northern Ireland before there could be any constitutional change there was again emphasised. The two men said that change would not be achieved by violence or by the threat of it; a renunciation of violence would, however, bring about an imaginative response from the two governments. Political initiatives would be a matter for those governments – implicit in this joint communiqué was that the Hume–Adams talks were being pushed to one side.

Gerry Adams responded on 1 November, by which time the Shankill bombing and what followed had sent everyone back to their trenches and Northern Ireland was once more buried in a pit of despair. Adams said that the joint Major–Reynolds communiqué had clearly rejected the process that he and John Hume were involved in without offering an obvious alternative. Adams pointed to the fact that on 3 October the leadership of the IRA had said that the Irish Peace Initiative could provide the basis for peace. He accused Major of having no real interest in developing a real peace process and said that the British prime minister could not and must not be permitted to reject this opportunity for peace. Adams said the response of the British government to the developing peace initiative had been inexcusably negative and dismissive: 'Major's dependancy on unionist votes has obviously been a significant factor and this has been a matter of serious concern for those involved in the peace initiative.' (At this time, the nine Ulster Unionist MPs at Westminster had come to an 'understanding' with the Conservative government – an understanding carved out between Major and the UUP leader James Molyneaux – which helped to prop up the government's slim Commons majority.) The Adams statement went on to say:

> There is an onerous responsibility on Mr Reynolds. It is obvious that the British government will seize upon any opportunity to divert attention from Major's reluctance to be part of a genuine peace process and in order not to be seen to have rejected an opportunity for a lasting peace. Let me assure Mr Reynolds that I am anxious to ensure that any proposals he may have will be given a fair hearing by republicans. At the same time he must be aware that the seriousness of the situation and recent events demand urgent action from his government to focus the attention of the British government on its responsibility to play a leading role in removing the causes of conflict and division in Ireland. An endeavour by Mr Reynolds to do this would have my support. No one can be allowed to play propaganda games with a situation as serious as the one we are all faced with. Two weeks ago, I pointed out that we are at a crossroads in our history. An opportunity to create a real peace process clearly does exist. This requires courage and imagination particularly on the part of the two governments.

Republican concerns were highlighted in a statement from the IRA leadership on 2 November. That statement said the IRA had noted the British prime minister's rejection of the Irish Peace Initiative: 'We are concerned that this rejection, far from being the forerunner of an alternative peace initiative, is in fact the forerunner of a counter-insurgency offensive. This has not worked before and will not bring peace in the future.' The IRA then repeated that it welcomed the Hume–Adams initiative and that it had been informed of the broad principles involved. The statement said it was unfortunate that the British government's response had been 'negative' but repeated that 'if the political will and courage exist or can be created then this could provide the basis for peace'. The IRA said it and its supporters and activists had a 'vested interest in seeing peace and justice in Ireland', and the statement repeated republican objectives including the right of the Irish people to self-determination.

By early November, something of a political somersault seemed to have occurred in Dublin. It was being reported in the wake of the Fianna Fáil ard-fheis that the Hume–Adams initiative had been revived as a result of its popularity among grassroots nationalists. Because of the sensitivities that still attach to the peace process, more than six months after the ceasefires neither John Hume nor Gerry Adams was prepared to discuss their views on how Dublin behaved during this period, but there is a sense within republicanism that between June and December 1993 the British government managed to take the Dublin government away from the Hume–Adams initiative and move it to the position it took in the Downing Street Declaration. Meantime, after the slaughter on the Shankill and at Greysteel there was a relative lull in violent activity. The IRA murdered a police officer in an attack in Newry in early November, one in a series of shootings in the area of Newry and south Armagh in which members of the security forces were killed in single-shot sniper attacks. Also in November, the UFF murdered a Catholic factory worker at Dundonald on the outskirts of east Belfast.

Republicans also continued their verbal assault on the British government. On 14 November, at a Sinn Féin convention in Belfast, Martin McGuinness said the British prime minister must face up to the fact that the Hume–Adams initiative 'is the only process before us capable of moving us in the direction of peace'. The Derry republican also emphasised the IRA's support for the initiative and said he believed its 'positive attitude' was durable. In reference to that recent political about-turn in Dublin, he said that the government there had responded to a 'positive and supportive public mood'. His message for John Major, he said, was that the Irish people would have peace: 'Regardless of your sordid little deal with the unionists – or unionist manipulation of the British-sponsored veto – regardless of your rejection of the most imaginative and bold political initiative in twenty-five years, we the Irish people will have peace and we will have real peace.'

McGuinness is hugely influential within republicanism, and within a fortnight of his Belfast speech, he would move to centre-stage as another political drama began to unfold. It began with persistent rumours of secret contacts between the British government and the republican leadership – rumours which had been robustly dismissed by the Northern Ireland Office and Downing Street. The Belfast journalist Eamonn Mallie first floated the story, and on 16 November, he and I reported a claim that at the republican end of the contact Martin McGuinness had been the key figure. Days later, Mallie would produce documentary proof to substantiate his original report and by the weekend of 27–28 November the contacts were exposed and admitted. McGuinness, who as a young republican had been part of an IRA delegation that met the then Northern Ireland secretary of state, William Whitelaw, way back in July 1972, had indeed been the key republican figure in these latest secret exchanges between the two sides some two decades later.

7

WHISPERING IN THE SHADOWS

In the run-up to the exposure of the contacts between the British government and republicans there had been all sorts of whispering in the sidelines. A version of events outlined to me suggested the contacts had been cleared at the highest level on both sides and that they had spanned a considerable period of time. Documents had been exchanged and the contacts had overlapped the Hume–Adams dialogue. This account of events was given to me by a source who had been reliable over a period of many years and I ran the details of the briefing in a television news report on 16 November 1993. In this piece I also reported the claim that Martin McGuinness had been the key figure at the republican end of the secret exchanges. This report followed on the heels of a statement issued by the Sinn Féin president, Gerry Adams, late on 15 November. That night the British prime minister, John Major, had used a speech at London's Guildhall to focus on Northern Ireland – a speech that angered Adams and that prompted the first on-the-record claim of contacts between the republican leadership and the British government.

Major told his Guildhall audience that there 'may now be a better opportunity for peace in Northern Ireland than for many years'. He spoke of several important elements coming together and said there was a burning desire on each side of the community for peace: not a peace at any price but a peace that was fair and just. Major said his government would work to protect all the people of Northern Ireland and Britain from terrorism and to convince the men of violence in both communities to end violence unconditionally and for ever and to choose instead the path of legimate and democratic political activity.

'Some would deny them that path on account of their past and present misdeeds. I understand that feeling but I do not share it. Let me tonight make explicit what has always been implicit. Those who decline to renounce violence can never have a place at the conference table in our democracy, but if the IRA end violence for good then after a sufficient interval to ensure the permanence of their intent Sinn Féin can enter the political arena as a democratic party and join the dialogue on the way ahead. There can be no secret deals, no rewards for terrorists, no abandonment of the vital principle of majority consent but there is the incentive: the incentive that peace would bring a new and far better way of life to all the people of that troubled land.'

The prime minister was setting out in crystal-clear terms the conditions under which Sinn Féin could enter talks. The IRA would first have to end its campaign of violence; a period of quarantine would then follow to ensure that this was genuine and permanent. This was also another clear government statement that any constitutional change would require majority consent in Northern Ireland. Republicans were not impressed and indeed Gerry Adams was said to be furious. That night, I took a call at home from Richard McAuley. The purpose of his call was to pass on a statement from Adams, a statement in which he said representatives of Sinn Féin had been 'in protracted contact and dialogue with the British government'. 'It was John Major who broke off that contact at the behest of his unionist allies. This evening's speech is to deflect attention from this. Mr Major cannot dodge his responsibility so easily. He must grasp the opportunity for peace, not play politics with it. The British and Irish people deserve better.'

On 18 November, Martin McGuinness also went on the record: 'I can confirm that I was involved in direct and protracted contact and dialogue with the British government. This contact was at an official level and no preconditions were set upon it. Sinn Féin is quite ready to engage in talks at any time to create the conditions in which a peace process can be constructed and a political settlement reached.' By now it seemed that a huge story was on the verge of breaking. Republicans were emphasising that Gerry Adams and Martin McGuinness would not be making these claims unless they could prove them but no admission of involvement was forthcoming from the government side and it would take another week or so before the story would finally be smoked out.

In between times there was another Hume–Adams statement and, in an interview in the republican weekly newspaper *An Phoblacht*, the IRA gave details of its current thinking. Some weeks earlier, the prime minister had told the SDLP leader that the Hume–Adams agreement was not the right way to proceed, but despite this, Hume and Adams said in their statement on 20 November they hoped the British government would respond 'positively and quickly to the clear opportunity for peace which this initiative provides'.

> The most pressing issue facing the people of Ireland and Britain, as now appears to be agreed by all sides, is the question of a lasting peace and how it can best be achieved. We are personally greatly encouraged by the popular and widespread support which has greeted the initiative and by the many personal messages of support and encouragement that we have received. We remain committed to this peace initiative and to the creation of a peace process which would involve both governments and all parties. We also remain convinced, despite all the difficulties, that a process can be designed to lead to agreement among the divided people of this island which will provide a solid basis for peace. We are examining ways to advance the initiative. We have taken no decision on the publication of the substance of the initiative, the objectives of which have been made clear in our previous statements.

John Hume and Gerry Adams quite clearly were not prepared to take no for an answer.

Within days the IRA again outlined its position on the initiative:

> The Hume–Adams initiative has acted as a major catalyst forcing many people, in some cases for the first time, to seriously address

the question of how we move from a situation of conflict towards a position where we lay the foundations of a peace process which removes the causes of conflict and provides a political framework for a negotiated settlement and lasting peace.

Questioned on Dublin's handling of the process, the IRA said that Albert Reynolds 'should never have given the leeway he did with the Brussels communiqué'. 'Dublin knows what is required. It should seek to move the British to that position.' The IRA described as 'hypocritical nonsense' preconditions being set on Sinn Féin's entry into talks given that the British government 'were in protracted contact and dialogue with Sinn Féin representatives until the British side ended the dialogue earlier this year. We for our part were kept fully informed of all the details of this and we have every confidence in the Sinn Féin leadership to conduct this and any other dialogue they are engaged in.' When confirmation of the contacts came it was revealed that Martin McGuinness and Gerry Kelly, a convicted bomber who escaped from the Maze jail in the 1983 IRA breakout, were the republicans involved. In that IRA interview in *An Phoblacht* it was stated that the right of the Irish people to national self-determination and the question of lasting peace were 'inextricably linked': 'We seek a real peace process and support the present [Hume–Adams] one. We do not expect John Major to call a unilateral halt to British military activity in Ireland. He knows there can be no unilateral halt by us. There needs to be a negotiated settlement. We want peace. No one should doubt our determination.'

In the same week of this interview the loyalist terrorist leadership spoke of exploring the prospects for peace while at the same time 'preparing for war', and, on the eve of that IRA interview, a huge arms shipment destined for the Ulster Volunteer Force was intercepted at Teesport in England. On board the freighter, which had sailed from Poland, customs officers uncovered more than 300 rifles, handguns, ammunition, grenades, detonators and two tons of high explosive. That afternoon, in the Shankill area of Belfast, I met three men in a darkened room. The man who did most of the talking wore a cap and glasses and had the collar of his coat turned up. He told me there was no need for introductions. A brown envelope had been placed on a table in the room and I was asked to remove a sheet of paper from it. It was a statement from the UVF leadership, which read as follows:

> We, the Ulster Volunteer Force, in claiming responsibility for the arms seized in England wish to make it clear to the people of Ulster that whilst it is a logistical setback, it in no way diminishes our ability nor our determination to carry on the war against the IRA. The spirit of 1912 and the *Clyde Valley* lives on. It is a heritage too proud to be cynically manipulated by political quislings nor brutally cowed by military means. For so long as we are in receipt of the support of the loyalist people, in whatever form, so we will continue to put at risk our volunteers to scour the world for arms to be used in their defence and for that of our country. We would ask them in these dark days to continue that support in the sure and certain knowledge that we will remain unbowed and unbroken.

In reality the UVF's preparations for war had suffered a serious setback. That organisation had long been trying to get its hands on commercial explosive in order to be able to match the IRA's bombing capability. Indeed, during my research for this book, a UVF leadership source admitted as much: 'Teesport was about equalising the situation – putting our own forces on a level playing field.' This source remained adamant, however, that the seizure of the consignment amounted to nothing more than a logistical setback: 'What can be got once can be got again.' My information is that the weapons shipped from Poland were never going to get through to Belfast. I understand that the original intelligence information which led to a surveillance operation came from the RUC. They had watched this arms smuggling plot begin to unfold in the early part of 1993. The weapons cost the UVF a substantial six-figure sum and were paid for in two instalments. All this was monitored and a decision was taken not to allow the shipment to run beyond Britain.

Meanwhile, as the weekend of 27–28 November approached,

the British government knew the story of its secret contacts with the republican leadership was going to run again, only this time there would be no denials. Documentary proof in the shape of an *aide-mémoire* used by an intermediary while delivering a government document to Martin McGuinness in March 1993 had been obtained by Eamonn Mallie and the government's cover was blown. Mallie supplied the *Observer* with the details and ahead of its report on Sunday 28 November a statement was issued by the NIO. This statement, dated 27 November, contained a most remarkable claim:

> At the end of February this year a message was passed on to the government from the IRA leadership. It was to the effect that the conflict was over but they needed our advice as to the means of bringing it to a close. The government obviously had to take that message seriously, though we recognised that actions not words would be the real test. The government had already made it publicly clear what had to be done by those who used or threatened violence for political ends. If they wanted to enter into talks or negotiations with the government, there first had to be a genuine ending of violence. The government accordingly responded to the IRA's request for advice. The response reinforced and spelt out in a private message what the government had consistently said publicly. There had first of all to be a genuine end to violence. It also repeated the constitutional guarantee.

At a Stormont news conference the following morning the Northern Ireland secretary of state Sir Patrick Mayhew said that message had been sent by Martin McGuinness.

At that news conference, I asked Sir Patrick how in February anyone could have had the impression that the conflict was coming to an end when that very month the IRA had killed five people – four of them security force members and the fifth an alleged police informant – and since then had continued to bomb and shoot. He replied by saying that was a good question to put to the IRA and he went on to add: 'I have a responsibility for the lives of people in Northern Ireland and if I receive a message by a well-established chain of communication coming from the leadership of the IRA that the conflict is over but we need advice as to how to bring it to an end, I am not going to pass that up. I recognised, of course, as did my colleagues, that it is actions and not words that will be the ultimate test. I said that in the statement yesterday but I was prepared and was obliged in duty to the people of Northern Ireland to deal with that message on the assumption that it was serious. That is what I did.' I then asked him if he had the impression that this was an unconditional end to violence that was being talked about and he replied yes: 'I certainly did. The message said the conflict is over but we need your British advice as to how to bring it to a close. Any invitation to bargain would have been dismissed out of hand and in my reply as I have read to you [reporters at the news conference] I stated the British government's position is very clear.' My next question related to that interview I had done with Martin McGuinness in March 1993 in which he had said there would be no unilateral IRA move, that a formula would have to be found in which the two sides moved at the same time and that even if there were to be talks between the government and republicans there would be no guarantee of an end to armed struggle. I asked again how could anyone at that time have been of the impression that republicans were considering an unconditional move.

In his answer, Mayhew said that this was his clear understanding of the message. 'Well if you get a message saying the conflict is over and we want advice as to how it is to be brought to a close you have two choices. One is to say they can't mean it, in which event you have to answer to people when there is a subsequent outrage, no less inexcusable than all the rest, you have to answer to people as to why you brushed aside and took no action upon a message of that kind. That's what you have to do, and the other choice is to say, very well, actions will count louder than words, but you say, you're asking for advice, here it is. I chose the latter. I don't believe that most people in Northern Ireland would say that was wrong.' I followed up this answer from Sir Patrick by asking him had he heard what Martin McGuinness had had to say in March: 'I can't remember whether I heard at this moment in time what Martin McGuinness said then but I don't mind saying to you now that that message came from Martin McGuinness.'

That afternoon Gerry Adams responded to the secretary of state and said at no point was there any communication from the IRA that the 'conflict is over'. He said during the contacts outlines of policy were exchanged and discussed and that the British government had rejected and walked away from a peace process [Hume–Adams]. He accused the prime minister and the secretary of state of consistently telling lies about 'a number of matters central to the Irish Peace Initiative'. 'They have lied to their own Parliament, to Jim Molyneaux and to the Irish and British people about the existence and nature of their contact with Sinn Féin. Now that they have been forced to admit talking to Sinn Féin they are continuing to lie about what is involved; about the nature of the contact; about the IRA's position and about Sinn Féin's role. These lies and the patent dishonesty of the British position make a difficult situation worse. How can we make progress when they behave in this manner?' The Sinn Féin president accused the government of attempting to cause confusion.

On Monday 29 November Sir Patrick made a statement to Parliament and then lodged in the House of Commons library his record of the oral and written messages said to have been passed up and down the chain of contact through intermediaries. According to the government, the February 1993 communication stating that the conflict was over took the form of an oral message recorded by the Northern Ireland Office as such: 'The conflict is over but we need your advice on how to bring it to a close. We wish to have an unannounced ceasefire in order to hold dialogue leading to peace. We cannot announce such a move as it will lead to confusion for the volunteers because the press will misinterpret it as a surrender. We cannot meet the secretary of state's public renunciation of violence, but it would be given privately as long as we were sure that we were not being tricked.' This was said to have been passed to the government along with the text of speeches given to the Sinn Féin ard-fheis by Martin McGuinness and Gerry Adams.

That same day I interviewed Gerry Adams after a Sinn Féin news conference at Conway Mill in west Belfast, an interview in which he again categorically denied that the February message was sent. He also said that during the contacts the British government was kept informed of developments in the talks between himself and John Hume; Adams said republicans had been told that in talks between republican and British government delegations republicans 'would be shown that there was no longer any need for armed struggle'. The contacts, according to the Sinn Féin president, had stretched back long before the date given by Mayhew of February 1993.

'I don't even know where he gets February from. The current phase of dialogue and contact has been off and on for a number of years. There were exchanges of information and so on before February. Never at any time was there any communication from the IRA that the conflict was over and it needed advice on how to end its campaign. That is a blatant lie, and not only that, it is an attempt to mischieviously use this line, and I stress this line has never been abused by either party since it was established; a blatant attempt to disinform, to confuse and to, in a counter-insurgency way, save Mr Mayhew's neck.'

In his next answer the Sinn Féin leader disclosed that an IRA ceasefire had been sought and approved in May 1993: 'There was an exchange of documents; an exchange of policy documents, let me say; more so than the normal exchange of documents and in the course of this the British government proposed that there be a phase – a period – of delegation meetings; that is of a Sinn Féin delegation and the British government delegation coming together for a week, ten days, a fortnight, for an intense negotiation and discussion, and the British government asserted that in the course of this that republicans would be shown that there was no longer any need for armed struggle. They made it clear that such an assertion by them would be proved in the course of that discussion. We discussed venues, discussed timescales and privately in Sinn Féin discussed our delegation and in fact appointed a small secretariat.'

I then asked had any preconditions been set by the British side.

'There were no preconditions but the British government said that obviously it would be difficult if this was conducted against a background of an intense IRA campaign and we in Sinn Féin were faced with a moral dilemma. So, because of the British assertion and because of our commitment to seeking a peace process, we went to the leadership of the Irish Republican Army and they responded, in my view, generously to the British request and we conveyed, we in Sinn Féin conveyed, to the British that the IRA would suspend its operations for two weeks in order to permit us to best explore their position and that response, the IRA response to the British, was conveyed to them on 10 May.'

Why then did the meetings not take place?

'Well, I think the British government just walked away and I can only speculate on this but it is not a coincidence that this occurred at a time when the Major government was going into difficulties; the Maastricht debate was pending, there was the problem with its own right wing, Major himself was in some difficulties with cabinet colleagues. I actually can't remember all the detail of that, but he had difficulties with his own party and difficulties within the House of Commons and it looked like he was going to become dependent upon, if he was going to stay in power, become dependent on the votes of the Unionists.'

On the particular aspect of the contacts, the IRA spoke of the British government making a definitive proposal in March 1993 for 'full-blown delegate meetings' between its representatives and Sinn Féin. It also claimed that the government side had suggested possible venues for these meetings including Scotland and a number of Scandinavian countries:

A short unannounced suspension of IRA activity was requested by the British government to help accommodate these meetings. In response to this request, conveyed to us by the Sinn Féin representative, Oglaigh na h-Eireann [the IRA] decided that operations could be suspended for a two-week period. This was conveyed to the British government on May 10th. It is for John Major and his Cabinet to explain why they failed to deliver their proposal.

In this statement the IRA also said it refuted what it called the 'preposterous claim' by the London government that a message had been communicated that the conflict was over and advice was being sought on how to bring it to a close.

The unfolding story of the secret exchanges captured the attention of the media not just in Britain and Ireland but also internationally. For several days cameras and microphones were pointed at anything that moved in respect of this breaking news item. On 30 November, Gerry Adams said that an initial study of the material published by Sir Patrick Mayhew had shown there were a number of bogus documents and that changes had been made to others. He accused the British government of acting in bad faith and of abusing the contact between the two sides in order to sow dissension and confusion. All of this, he said, was devaluing the peace process. Martin McGuinness said that the government had invented a pretext in order to justify its contacts with republicans; the February message attributed to him and suggesting an IRA surrender was bogus, and the exchanges pre-dated February 1993. He said a British document passed to him after the Warrington bombs was not a reaction to a message that the conflict was over but something that was sent in response to speeches at that year's Sinn Féin ard-fheis.

In summing up this extraordinary period I think it is worth while pinpointing the key claims and counterstatements. For its part, the British government had started out by vigorously denying the contacts story and by rubbishing reports to the contrary. However, when the story was finally proved beyond all reasonable doubt the government tried to explain away its original denials on the grounds of having to ensure confidentiality and protect the lives of those involved in the secret chain of communication. The government stuck to its line that a message, effectively amounting to an IRA surrender, had been passed to it in February 1993; during its contacts with the Provisional leadership, the government said, it emphasised its publicly stated position that before talks or negotiations there would first have to be a permanent end to violence. The government admitted to around twenty errors in its published record of the contacts, some of them in key documents, and it suggested that face-to-face contacts between a British official and Martin McGuinness had been 'unauthorised'. Sir Patrick Mayhew survived the storm but was accused by Ian Paisley in Parliament of lying, a charge which led to the DUP leader being suspended from the Commons.

On the other side of the coin, republicans have categorically denied that the February message was sent and they say that at one stage in the contacts it was proposed that an unannounced two-week suspension of IRA activity would lead to delegation meetings with a British negotiating team. The contacts, according to republicans, stretched back to 1990; Sinn Féin says it was informed of the detail of the talks process involving both governments and the constitutional political parties in Northern Ireland. The unauthorised contacts referred to by the government were, according to republicans, authorised.

I discussed this period with Martin McGuinness in March 1995 at his home in Derry. In his front room we drank coffee and discussed for about an hour the importance of the contacts and how they fitted into what was known as the peace process. He explained to me that in terms of trying to resolve the conflict the exchanges between the two sides were of secondary importance and that in themselves they could not have provided the basis for any peace settlement. What was needed was all-inclusive talks involving both governments and all parties and in this context the Irish Peace Initiative and how it was developing was the issue of primary importance for republicans. The contacts with Britain, however, had provided Sinn Féin with valuable political intelligence on its opponents; McGuinness is of the view that republicans gained more than the British side from the exchanges. On the issue of the February message I asked him could anything sent up the chain of communication at that time have been misunderstood or confused, but he said there was no confusion; the message did not exist in written or in oral form.

At the end of what unfolded in that November–December 1993 period many people were inclined to believe the republican version of events, and the government's credibility had been seriously damaged by the way it had handled, or mishandled, the whole affair. By first denying the contacts and then changing tack the government had placed itself at a disadvantage; people felt misled, and William McCrea, the Democratic Unionist MP who had provided Eamonn Mallie with the documentary proof to substantiate the contacts story, said that both Major and Mayhew should resign. Ulster, he said, was in its greatest hour of crisis and the government could not be trusted.

Within a few weeks of all this, the loyalist terrorist leadership issued a policy statement. That statement from the Combined Loyalist Military Command came on 10 December and was given to me at a meeting in the Shankill area. The document gave details of a set of principles and its text read as follows:

> We wish to state our basic principles so that there may be no doubt in any quarter as to our deadly seriousness in pursuance of these ideals.
>
> 1 There must be no diminution of Northern Ireland's position as an integral part of the United Kingdom whose paramount responsibility is the morale and physical well-being of all its citizens.
>
> 2 There must be no dilution of the democratic procedure through which the rights of self-determination of the people of Northern Ireland are guaranteed.
>
> 3 We defend the right of anyone or group to seek constitutional change by democratic, legitimate and peaceful means.

4 We recognise and respect the rights and aspirations of all who abide by the law regardless of religious, cultural, national or political inclinations.

5 We are dedicated to a written constitution and bill of rights for Northern Ireland wherein would be enshrined stringent safeguards for individuals, associations and minorities.

6 Structures should be devised whereby elected representatives, North and South, could work together to explore and exploit co-operation between both parts of Ireland which would not interfere with either's internal jurisdiction.

It is our earnest desire to have an honourable and equitable peace founded in democratic accountable structures within which all of our people can play a constructive and meaningful role without let or hindrance. The shameful point-scoring of the past and present must be forever left behind us if we are to take our rightful place in a changing world. We must learn to accommodate each other's culture and tradition with a view to building that modern society which we all desire. Loyalist paramilitaries have been in active existence for many years with mercurial support from the general unionist population. Therefore we offer a word of caution to all those who are engaged in negotiative dialogue concerning Ulster's future. Get it right or the nominal support we now have will very quickly become total.

The loyalist leadership was setting out its stall and making clear that it would not tolerate any change in the constitutional status of Northern Ireland within the United Kingdom. It was also making clear that while cross-border co-operation could be explored it should not take any institutionalised shape in terms of joint authority over Northern Ireland by the British and Irish governments.

The Downing Street Declaration which followed five days later took the form of an agreed statement by the British and Irish prime ministers. The published document ran to twelve paragraphs and in the fourth of those, John Major, on behalf of his government, reaffirmed that they would uphold the democratic wish of a greater number of the people of Northern Ireland on the issue of whether they preferred to support the Union or a sovereign united Ireland, and he reiterated on the behalf of the British government that it had no 'selfish, strategic or economic interest in Northern Ireland', thus echoing the words of the former Northern Ireland secretary of state Peter Brooke. The paragraph went on to say that the primary interest was to see peace, stability and reconciliation established by agreement:

> The role of the British government will be to encourage, facilitate and enable the achievement of such agreement over a period through a process of dialogue and co-operation based on full respect for the rights and identities of both traditions in Ireland. They accept that such agreement may, as of right, take the form of agreed structures for the island as a whole, including a united Ireland achieved by peaceful means on the following basis. The British government agree that it is for the people of the island of Ireland alone, by agreement between the two parts respectively, to exercise their right of self-determination on the basis of consent, freely and concurrently given, North and South, to bring about a united Ireland, if that is their wish. They reaffirm as a binding obligation that they will, for their part, introduce the necessary legislation to give effect to this, or equally to any measure of agreement on future relationships in Ireland which the people living in Ireland may themselves freely so determine without external impediment. They believe that the people of Britain would wish, in friendship to all sides, to enable the people of Ireland to reach agreement on how they may live together in harmony and in partnership, with respect for their diverse traditions, and with full recognition of the special links and the unique relationship which exists between the peoples of Britain and Ireland.

In paragraph five Albert Reynolds, on behalf of the Irish government, said the lessons of Irish history had shown that stability and well-being would not be found under any political system that was refused allegiance or rejected on grounds of identity by a significant minority of those governed by it:

> For this reason, it would be wrong to attempt to impose a united Ireland, in the absence of the freely given consent of a majority of

the people of Northern Ireland. He [the taoiseach] accepts, on behalf of the Irish government, that the democratic right of self-determination by the people of Ireland as a whole must be achieved and exercised with and subject to the agreement and consent of a majority of the people of Northern Ireland.

Later in the declaration, both governments said they accepted that Irish unity could only be achieved 'by those who favour this outcome persuading those who do not, peacefully and without coercion or violence, and that, if in the future a majority of the people of Northern Ireland are so persuaded, both governments will support and give legislative effect to their wish'.

The then Northern chairman of Sinn Féin, Mitchel McLaughlin, gave the initial republican reaction to the declaration. He said the mood within his community was one of let-down and disappointment. He said Sinn Féin would, however, study the document and measure it against the Hume–Adams initiative, which, he said, had on three occasions received support from the IRA. (The definitive republican response would come much later, after months of wrangling over clarification, and following a special Sinn Féin conference in Letterkenny, County Donegal.) In that conversation I had with Gerry Adams in March 1995 he described the declaration as a 'crisis statement': 'I myself think that the Downing Street Declaration quite clearly was almost a crisis statement because a head of steam was building up. Hume–Adams, as it's called, was very popular in Ireland. Many people, universally and in Britain, recognised it as something significant. John Hume brought a standing to it and you had this marriage of my republican credentials being married to John Hume's international credentials. It was seen as having some sort of credibility. The Downing Street Declaration, I think somebody said at the time, was an attempt to stop both governments getting into confrontation.'

But unionists saw no credibility whatsoever in the Hume–Adams process. Indeed, the UUP leader James Molyneaux used words such as 'preposterous' and 'fiendish' to express his feelings about it. The Westminster MP Ken Maginnis told me that the verbal reassurances given to unionists by John Hume and Gerry Adams had never been reinforced by any offer of practical co-operation within the context of Northern Ireland. He said the secrecy surrounding the content of the Hume–Adams agreement and the refusal of republicans to accept the Downing Street Declaration had left unionists deeply suspicious about 'the real understanding between the two men'.

Despite what Gerry Adams said about the declaration being a 'crisis statement', it did win wide support in Ireland and Britain, and also internationally. It is for that reason that the RUC Chief Constable Sir Hugh Annesley believes it boxed republicans into a corner.

Two days after the publication of the declaration the first loyalist response came and with it an indication that their violence would continue. A statement from the CLMC said it would be looking at the document in the context of the set of principles it had recently outlined. The full text of its statement read:

> We are in receipt of the recent joint declaration issued by the British and Irish governments, the contents of which are being studied and analysed at this moment in time in conjunction with the principles issued by the Combined Loyalist Military Command on 10th December 1993. A comprehensive response will be made in due course after clarification on certain issues has been sought and received. In the interim period, and in the absence of any response from the Provisional murder gangs, the Combined Loyalist Military Command will pursue its stated policy in relation to IRA violence. In order to allay immediate loyalist fears and to maximise unionist unity, the Combined Loyalist Military Command calls for a forum to be instituted to encompass all the loyalist and unionist political parties in Ulster.

The CLMC was stressing that the political voice of loyalism should be heard in this type of forum, or indeed in any talks about the future of Northern Ireland.

Two weeks later, on 31 December, one of the loyalist groups gave a more detailed response to the declaration. In a statement the UFF said that both it and the leadership of the UDA had been engaged 'in a careful, detailed deliberation' of the declaration's contents. The statement said the views of outside advisers had also been sought and that the initial response to the document was one of 'scepticism'. The UFF said the declaration, despite its reference to consent freely given, had a wider agenda and had ignored 'the reality that the status of Northern Ireland within the United Kingdom was dramatically changed with the imposition of the Anglo-Irish Dictat [the Anglo-Irish Agreement of 1985]. The final two sentences of the statement read:

> The UDA and UFF exist because the government has abdicated its responsibility to protect the Northern Ireland state and its citizens. So long as the pan-nationalist terror and political coercion continues, we retain the right to respond militarily in 1994.

Just days into the New Year, the Presbyterian minister Roy Magee, who had been attempting to achieve an end to loyalist violence, organised a conference at a venue in east Belfast with the purpose of having the declaration explained to the paramilitary leadership. There was confusion because the two main unionist parties, the UUP and the DUP, had taken up entirely different positions on the document. The conference was held under the cover of the Concerned Loyalist Management Committee to shield the fact that many of the Combined Loyalist Military Command were present. The Ulster Unionists sent a representative along, party councillor and executive member Michael McGimpsey, but the DUP failed to take up its invitation. When I interviewed Councillor McGimpsey some days after the conference, on 2 February, and after I had disclosed details of it on the BBC's *Spotlight* programme, he said he had not been aware before the meeting that paramilitaries would be present, but he said that even had he known in advance he would still have attended: 'I was invited along to a seminar of leading loyalists of, I understood, a political nature, whose opinions, as I understood it, were of importance within the loyalist community.' He said he was aware of the post-declaration confusion caused by the dichotomy of views being put across by the unionist parties: 'On the one hand we are telling people to be calm; that the declaration is not a sell-out; that it is not placing anyone in a last-resort situation, and that, therefore, reactions of a violent nature are entirely inappropriate. On the other hand the DUP are telling people that it's a sell-out – with references to traitors, reaping whirlwinds and so on.' As far as Michael McGimpsey was concerned the conference provided a platform for explanation; he was not negotiating and, therefore, he said there were no parallels between what he was doing and the Hume–Adams talks. The councillor said the important thing was 'getting across a point of view to individuals who can make a difference, in effect, as far as levels of violence in Northern Ireland are concerned – and that's important'.

Ulster Unionist Party headquarters also defended its decision to be represented at the conference and issued the following statement in the name of the party's general secretary, Jim Wilson:

> We have a duty to take such action as is necessary to reassure and stabilise the community especially when some leading politicians are engaged in activity which causes instability. The Ulster Unionist Party held three regional meetings to brief its councillors and senior officials throughout the Province a number of weeks ago. They are now equipped to pass on the party's view to the wider community. Following these meetings the party was invited to send a representative to a seminar which was to be attended by academics, people with a legal background and loyalists concerned about the Joint Declaration. The representative would, it was said, be asked to address the seminar for about an hour on the Ulster Unionist Party's attitude to the declaration and wider issues. It would have been abnormal for the party not to send a speaker as such invitations routinely meet with a positive response. In this case an Ulster Unionist councillor attended and addressed the seminar.

The 'comprehensive' response the loyalist terrorist leadership had promised after the declaration never really materialised.

Indeed, after the two-day conference in east Belfast, only a brief statement was issued by the CLMC. It said it would not be giving a 'definitive' response to what was, in its view, an 'indefinitive' document. The full text of its statement read as follows:

> The declaration is a work of some ingenuity. After prolonged consultation with various prominent politicians, lawyers, constitutional lawyers and academics we have come to the conclusion we cannot have a definitive response to an indefinitive document. We neither accept nor reject it. To a large degree we are in a wait and see syndrome. The implementation of the document will be crucial. Consequently it is heavily incumbent upon the unionist parties to employ the same resilience and political acumen which they have shown hitherto.

Michael McGimpsey had made an impression at the east Belfast conference. Sources close to the UVF leadership described his explanation of the declaration as 'highly impressive, convincing and believeable', and the loyalist organisation decided that its 'active service units' would not be sent out to 'oppose' the joint statement by the two governments. With IRA violence continuing, however, there was still no prospect of loyalists ending their campaign.

8

GOING TO THE EDGE

The months of 1994 would be the most important in the history of modern republicanism – a time when the movement's key strategists would have to make fine judgements and balance the worth of armed struggle against the potential for political progress. Gerry Adams argues that the ceasefire declaration of 31 August 1994 took 'remarkable courage' given that from the IRA's point of view it placed its whole 'struggle' on the edge. The decision was unquestionably a remarkable one in that it represented a unilateral cessation – an illogical step in itself given all that had been said in the past by republican leaders and the political equivalent, if you like, of the cow actually jumping over the moon. Republicans, however, see the ceasefire as an initiative linked to political developments which may or may not bring a final resolution to this conflict. The strategy, they admit, is a high-risk one and no one knows how things will work out. The IRA statement on 31 August 1994 emerged from a process of slow, detailed consultation not just within the ranks of republicanism but involving others. Indeed, Gerry Adams says it has to be seen in the context of three statements from Irish-America, from himself and John Hume and from the taoiseach Albert Reynolds in the immediate period before the ceasefire announcement.

In the latter part of 1993 and in the months of 1994 there was a very clear tactical adjustment within the IRA's campaign. Its violence in that period was directed almost exclusively against the security forces, and incendiary devices replaced car bombs in attacks on 'economic targets'. In October 1993 the Shankill bombing had seriously damaged the 'peace process', and in this reworking of violent methods the risk of a similar 'blunder' occurring was being greatly reduced. When I discussed with Gerry Adams the period leading to the ceasefire, he spoke to me of knowing what makes the IRA 'tick', of knowing where it comes from, and in terms of its deliberations over the ceasefire he told me he would have understood whatever decision the IRA would have taken. That it came to the conclusions that it did had much to do with the type of arguments being put forward by Adams and by Martin McGuinness – two men whose influence over a period of two and a half decades had remodelled republicanism and reshaped its thinking. Republicans do not yet believe that the causes of the conflict as they see them have been removed, but they are on the agenda and republicans believe that a favourable political climate exists at present in which there is the potential and the possibility for progress. Whether enough progress can be made to satisfy them, however, and to ensure there is no return to the violent methods of the past, is another matter.

A look at how the IRA acted in the period after the Shankill bombing shows that tactical switch in its campaign. In the closing weeks of 1993 there were five more IRA killings and all five victims were members of the security forces. Three of them were killed in single-shot sniper attacks. As the year turned, there was still no indication of definite moves towards peace and at the start of 1994 several businesses in the greater Belfast area were destroyed in firebomb attacks – incidents which left behind a repair bill running into millons of pounds. The first IRA murder of the year happened on 17 February when a young RUC officer, Johnston Beacom, was killed in a rocket attack in the Markets area of Belfast. In the early part of the following month, an off-duty police officer was shot dead at a greyhound stadium in the north of the city. Around this time there were also attacks on Heathrow, where on three occasions in the space of five days between 9 and 13 March mortar bombs were launched at the airport. The devices did not explode but the IRA was demonstrating what it was capable of. If peace was coming there was not much evidence of it on the surface. But in a statement at this time the IRA said it remained 'positive and flexible' and there was a need for the British government 'to move from its current negative stance': the continued opportunity for peace should not be squandered.

At this time, Sinn Féin was still demanding clarification of the Downing Street Declaration from the British government and in late March I again interviewed Martin McGuinness to explore with him the republican analysis of the situation. On the issue of clarification he said he felt this could be cleared up in a couple of days and then a judgement could be made as to whether or not there were grounds for moving forward, but he stressed that republicans were not interested in the type of secret contact with Britain that had been the subject of so much controversy those few months earlier. Sinn Féin wanted its contact to be 'up front' and 'out in the open'. I asked him at what level he would expect this contact to take place, and he said at a level of the British government sending along people who could represent their point of view. Republicans would not set preconditions as to who these people should be: 'We're not, for example, looking for a meeting with the prime minister. What we're looking for is for the British government to recognise that we have a mandate, a democratic mandate, to represent people who have been oppressed and unjustly treated by different British and unionist regimes over the years. We're going to fight like lions to defend the right of those people to have their opinions listened to.' As we stood in Cable Street in the Bogside area of Derry chatting after the interview Martin McGuinness explained to me that his reference to fighting like lions was meant in the political sense. Given the twin strategy of republicanism he obviously felt the need to give some 'clarification' of his own.

At the time of the publication of the Downing Street Declaration the British prime minister had made clear that republicans could enter the democratic political process within three months of an end to the violence, and in that interview with Martin McGuinness I asked him for his views on this.

'I think there are many people out in the republican community who believe that what the British government is actually after is a defeat of republican resistance. Many people believe that the British government are trying to break the republican community once and for all.' I now sought some clarification of my own and asked him if republicans were of the view that what the British government were asking for was an IRA surrender: 'I think that there are many people within the republican community who believe that that's exactly what the British government are looking for.'

Martin McGuinness is seen as someone with a very clear read on all aspects of republican 'struggle', and therefore I asked him what evidence there was to support the IRA's claim that it was 'positive and flexible' – given the concerted series of attacks being directed against the security forces: 'Well, many republicans would believe that they result from Britain's unwillingness to become seriously involved in the peace process. I don't know if that is correct or not. The only people who can answer that is the British government.'

McGuinness said republicans were interested in laying the groundwork for a peace that could be permanent and he kept emphasising the need for clarification of the Downing Street Declaration. Albert Reynolds had provided this early on but the British government's stance was that the declaration was self-explanatory and that republicans were deliberately stalling. McGuinness denied this: 'They've thrown this at us for some time, for some months, that we are stalling the thing, that we're not serious about it, that we're not really looking to move forward and that we are insincere about the whole process. So what we say quite clearly to them – take it away from us. Let's have this meeting and then we'll see where we stand at the end of that process and all of this could be accomplished within the next week, or the next fortnight.'

A seventy-two-hour IRA Easter ceasefire, described by that organisation as a unilateral initiative, was announced within days, on 30 March, and came into effect at midnight on 5 April. In a statement the IRA said it hoped that the British government would accept this further opportunity in the spirit in which it was offered and that it would be used to the best advantage of the British and Irish people:

> Making peace is a difficult business for all involved but the difficulties must be overcome. That too is the responsibility of all involved but particularly the British government. We hope that the further opportunity here provided is used to that purpose and effect.

This development was welcomed by Gerry Adams, who called on John Major to authorise direct and immediate talks between British government representatives and Sinn Féin. At around the time of the IRA announcement the prime minister had arrived in Northern Ireland for a short visit and his reaction to the cessation was to describe it as a cynical public relations exercise. In Dublin, Albert Reynolds said he was disappointed that the ceasefire was for such a short period, but he did add that he was glad that it was unconditional and unilateral. Yet another view was given by the RUC Chief Constable, Sir Hugh Annesley, who described the shortness of the Easter ceasefire to me as derisory, but then added, 'I don't think it was deliberately intended at that stage just to be a three-day ceasefire by the leadership of PIRA. I suspect at that time it was all they felt they could get, but I think the condemnation both inside and outside Northern Ireland from all shades of opinion was quite staggering. I mean even the radio broadcast that morning asking people in the street what they felt must have carried a message back to the leadership of the republican movement.'

Despite the criticism of the Easter cessation those within republicanism saw it as significant. Given the different levels of political sophistication within that movement, small steps would have to come first. Easter 1994 meant that temporary ceasefires were once more an acceptable tactical option within the republican movement; the IRA, it seemed, had finally exorcised the ghosts of ceasefires past. During the ceasefires of the 1970s, republicans at the most senior level believed that Britain acted in bad faith. They also feared that ceasefires could damage the IRA beyond repair.

That is not to say that the delivery of this brief break in violence had been straightforward. Indeed, security sources told me that it brought 'massive complaint at grassroots level' within the IRA about a lack of consultation; this assessment says that internally it was a 'disaster' for the republican leadership in terms of how they had handled it. Again according to this assessment, the process from Easter right through to 31 August involved 'massive planning, massive consultation – a massive show of democracy on their part [the republican leadership's] to keep their people behind them'. The challenge for the leaders of republicanism during this period was to bring the 'critical mass' of their organisation along with them and to avoid a split at all costs.

The role of Gerry Adams in this whole evolving process was 'pivotal' and as he and others such as Martin McGuinness moved to persuade the broad republican movement of the political worth of an unarmed strategy they had majority backing from the IRA Army Council. Security sources admit that it is inconceivable that the ceasefire could have been delivered without Adams; according to this assessment he and McGuinness were 'the lead players' in the debate. For republicans there was a choice to be made. Was it to be a continuation of the IRA's 'long war' or would they travel the political path? Outside the ranks of republicanism the man best placed to read the mind of Gerry Adams was perhaps John Hume. He was convinced that if anyone could deliver an IRA cessation it was the Sinn Féin president, but he also knew that it would take time: 'That's why after Downing Street I was the one person who kept telling people to be patient because I realised that given the nature of their organisation that it had to be intensive dialogue involving every single member.' Any mishandling of the situation could have led to a split within republicanism and the consequences of that could have been lethal.

Intelligence information on the internal debate within republicanism was reaching the security forces at 'three discernible levels' in the months running from the Downing Street Declaration through to August 1994. At a leadership level within the republican movement there were those who were arguing that 'armed struggle' had run its course and that more could be achieved by going the political route. The aims and objectives of republicans would not change, the organisation would remain intact, munitions would not be handed over in case there was a need to return to violence, but the argument being put was that more progress could be made through unarmed struggle. This assessment was given to me by a senior security source and continued as follows: 'At a level lower than that you had people in mid and high positions saying it [the ceasefire] won't work, it can't work but we will be prepared to give it a chance on the proviso that we keep intact, we keep gathering intelligence, we keep meeting regularly and we retain our position that we reserve the right to hit back and hit back hard; and, at grassroots level, you had people saying, this is crazy.' At this level within the organisation, the feeling was that 'war' was all Britain understood. According to security sources the difficulty throughout this lengthy period and the reason the ceasefire took so long in coming was this whole process of consultation and persuasion that indeed the 'war' should be over. These sources made it clear that republicans had not suddenly come to believe that violence was morally wrong but that the debate within the movement had been won on the argument that 'more could be gained along an unarmed path'. In this process of internal scrutiny, republicans had come to the view that more progress could be made if they could win the backing of significant 'political forces' for a peace process. Critical to all of this was Irish-American opinion and the positions taken up by the Dublin government and by John Hume.

While the internal debate continued so too did IRA violence; this was still dominated by attacks on the security forces although there were also incidents which resulted in civilian deaths. On 24 April two Protestant men, alleged by the IRA to be members of the UFF, were shot dead in Garvagh, County Londonderry, but that claim by the IRA was dismissed by the loyalist group, which accused the IRA of trying to cover up and justify the random sectarian murder of Protestants. In the early hours of the following morning I would find myself covering the aftermath of what the IRA called an 'anti-drugs operation' – a series of shootings across Belfast in which one man was killed and sixteen others were wounded. The IRA called this a preliminary strike in an ongoing operation. The days of May would also bring more killings including the murder of Fred Anthony, who was a cleaner at an RUC station. His young daughter Emma was seriously injured in the incident and pictures of her fighting for her life in a hospital bed touched the hearts of the people of Northern Ireland. Fortunately she survived, but another family had been scarred for life. Two soldiers were also killed in May, one in an explosion; the other, a part-time member of the Royal Irish Regiment, was shot after being abducted. In June the IRA attempted to kill the prominent Portadown loyalist Billy Wright and weeks later shot dead Ray Smallwoods, a political adviser to the UDA leadership and one of loyalism's principal theorists. I learned in 1995, during my research for this book, that in the weeks leading up to this killing the CLMC had outlined its terms for a ceasefire in a document passed to two clergymen, the Presbyterian minister Roy Magee and the Church of Ireland Primate Dr Robin Eames (see Chapter 12).

Meanwhile, British clarification of the Downing Street Declaration had been given to Sinn Féin in a series of written answers in May and, as the party moved towards its special conference in Letterkenny in July, where it discussed the document, speculation about a ceasefire continued. Republican sources, however, were steering me away from expectations of such a development at this stage and were stressing that the necessary pieces of the jigsaw were not yet in place. This was another issue I discussed with Gerry Adams when we met in March 1995.

'Some of the media got themselves into a quandary that we mismanaged the media element of the Letterkenny conference. That isn't the case. We had hoped that the Letterkenny conference would have taken place in a climate where the statements which came on the direct eve of the IRA statement [of 31 August], that we would have had Albert Reynolds, John Hume, Irish-America making the type of contribution that they later did, but that was not possible for all of them to do that at the time of the Letterkenny conference. So we went into the Letterkenny conference knowing that as we came out of it – because the media had spun this as one where there was going to be this great breakthrough – we knew that there couldn't have been a breakthrough because the ingredients, the parts of the jigsaw, were not in place. That's why Albert Reynolds, who was aware of this, was able to take a different attitude than everybody else because he knew that it couldn't happen, that the media had it wrong, that it couldn't happen at that time. He knew why it couldn't happen and he probably had a fairly educated guess that it would happen because the people who were required to make a contribution were favourably disposed to doing that. So we knew we were going to get it on the chin after the Letterkenny conference because there was this false perception about what it was about.' It will emerge later that Gerry Adams gave the IRA a detailed briefing on his analysis of the political situation in the period leading to the Letterkenny conference.

At that conference, Sinn Féin highlighted what it considered to be 'negative and contradictory elements' within the Downing Street Declaration. While Britain had asserted that it had 'no selfish, strategic or economic interest in Northern Ireland', there had been no mention of Britain's 'political interests, selfish or otherwise'. The following points were also contained in motions passed by the conference:

● The British have no right to determine how we exercise the right to self-determination. This is a matter for the Irish people.

- Time and time again in the declaration the [unionist] veto is reiterated.

- The Downing Street Declaration is also replete with reassurances to the unionists which are nowhere matched by any recognition of the rights of nationalists.

- The denial of nationalist rights is not addressed in the Downing Street Declaration.

- Nationalists are locked into the British state against their wishes. Their consent was never sought.

- The right to give or withhold consent was not and is not extended to nationalists.

Republicans saw the declaration as part of a wider process and not as a solution. (This point was underscored in the IRA ceasefire statement when it eventually emerged at the end of August.) The declaration did, however, enjoy wide and significant international support.

In his comments to me in 1995 on the Letterkenny period, Gerry Adams mentioned Albert Reynolds: the Sinn Féin president believes that the then taoiseach brought an important quality to the peace process – a quality that centred on his ability to take decisions. Adams spoke to me of Britain having to deal with a Dublin taoiseach 'who was fit to say to them, I'm doing this, I'm doing that'. Certainly Reynolds was sending signals to the republican movement that it was worth their while pursuing a democratic political path. His government lifted the broadcasting ban on Sinn Féin in the Republic in January 1994, and through a chain of intermediaries he had agreed in advance that in the event of a complete end to violence there would be movement on the issue of what republicans call 'political prisoners' and he would meet Gerry Adams publicly within a week of an announced cessation. After my meeting with Gordon Wilson in Dublin on 2 February 1995, I spoke with Albert Reynolds for over an hour in his office in Leinster House. By this time he was no longer taoiseach, his government having fallen in a row linked to the handling of an extradition case involving a priest, and he was now able to talk that bit more freely. The Reynolds government had a network of intermediaries giving them a link to both communities in the North. To ensure confidentiality the project was confined to the taoiseach's office; his aide, Dr Martin Mansergh, played a vital part in this process. The clear message being sent to republicans focused on the need for an end to violence before real political progress could be made, but Reynolds knew they would first have to be persuaded of the worth of an unarmed strategy.

'I was well aware throughout from the very start that an alternative strategy would have to be put in place that would make it possible for the leadership of Sinn Féin to go to the IRA Army Council to try to convince them that there was an alternative route, a route through the democratic process that could produce results and that there was a vast amount of goodwill and support to be gathered around the world behind this new direction.' It was this type of thinking which prompted the taoiseach to take up a strong position in favour of Gerry Adams getting a visa to enter the United States in February 1994, a move the British government was opposed to. Albert Reynolds was demonstrating his willingness to be decisive, his willingness to use the influence of his office to persuade the US administration that the 'risk' of granting a visa was worth taking and he was doing this in the knowledge that Britain was opposed to such a move. But the taoiseach was also using his intermediaries to hammer home to republicans the price Dublin was seeking for its involvement in this process: a complete cessation of violence. Albert Reynolds had researched Adams: he spoke to me of watching him and of reading everything he had said going back over a number of years: 'I felt that there was a change of direction taking place and that he was trying to lead the republican movement into a peace process but first of all he had to be convinced that there was a future in the peace process.' The taoiseach said he knew the Sinn Féin president had to be able to demonstrate the worth of an alternative strategy 'and it was demonstrated on a number of occasions that what he had come looking for he was able to deliver, such as the visa to Washington, such as Section 31 [the dropping of the Republic's broadcasting ban on Sinn Féin].' Gerry Adams too told me that 'within reason' there was an agreement reached about how the process would develop. Adams says there were decisions that Albert Reynolds took in the course of that process that he would not agree with but, none the less, in his briefings to the IRA he argued that the Fianna Fáil/Labour coalition was the most favourably disposed to the process and that it was likely to be there for two years: 'In other words, you had a situation of a London and Dublin government which would be running at the same general timescale.' The fall of Albert Reynolds was not something that republicans could have foreseen and nor was it something they wanted to happen.

Even before Letterkenny, republicans had made clear that the Downing Street Declaration did not measure up to Hume–Adams, that it was not a solution but, so far as they were concerned, a piece in a jigsaw and their challenge emerging from the conference in County Donegal was to work to bridge the gap between the two, particularly on the issue of the exercise of the right to national self-determination. There was a depressing mood in the immediate wake of this conference, but that was lifted when private republican briefings began to point to the early prospect not just of a temporary ceasefire but of something more lasting.

On 2 August I was told of that briefing that Gerry Adams had given to the IRA leadership around the time of Letterkenny, a briefing at which he outlined what he thought was politically possible. I was told that the IRA had asked for this as part of its overall consideration of the peace process, and that evening the BBC reported exclusively the information emerging from this conversation. A statement from the IRA the following morning confirmed the detail of my report.

On 4 August, in another briefing, I was told that a ceasefire was something that was 'going to happen rather than might happen' and that although there would be no let-up in violence until an actual announcement, that did not 'change the potential that existed'. That continuing violence would claim the life of part-time RIR soldier Trelford Withers on 8 August. He was shot dead in his butcher's shop in Crossgar, County Down, and was the last victim of IRA violence before its ceasefire. Just days later, however, further hints of what was down the road came in an address by Gerry Adams at a republican rally at Belfast City Hall on Sunday 14 August. He said the Irish Peace Initiative had seen important advances made in the past two years, the core political issues in the republican mind were on the agenda and were being discussed and the potential in all of this was, he said, considerable. The crowd of several thousand heard Adams say he was confident that the peace process could move forward towards its goal of a negotiated political settlement: 'It will be difficult and dangerous, it will take time and as events unfold in the months ahead there will be the inevitable begrudgers, the doubters and the revisionists, those who were never for the peace process and who will tell us that it cannot succeed.' Later in his address he added these words: 'I am especially confident that after twenty-five years of unparalleled courage and self-sacrifice, the nationalist people of this part of Ireland are prepared to show the way to a new future while at the same time reaching out the hand of friendship to unionists.'

Every day now I was in contact with a range of sources spread through republicanism, loyalism, the security field and prisons – contacts designed to glean as much information as possible about the evolving situation. It was a situation spiked with many conflicting signals, for while the private republican briefings continued to point to a peace move of some sort, on the surface an altogether different impression was being formed. At the end of July two loyalists, Joe Bratty and Raymond Elder, were shot dead on the Ormeau Road in Belfast. Subsequently the IRA engaged in a series of bomb attacks on pubs in predominantly Protestant areas, attacks which hurt no one but none the less earned the scorn of loyalists and unionists. One of those pub bombings was in the south Belfast constituency of the Westminster MP Martin Smyth, who accused the IRA of reverting to the tactics of the 1970s. He warned that

Northern Ireland was facing an extremely dangerous time. In this period the IRA also shot dead a leading Dublin criminal, Martin Cahill, whom it accused of having links with militant loyalism and more specifically with a UVF unit it suspected had been involved in a gun and bomb attack on a pub in Dublin in which an IRA 'volunteer' was killed.

In this period I interviewed the security minister at Stormont, Sir John Wheeler, who made clear that while the government would welcome any let-up in the violence, talks could only follow from a permanent end to the killing; any temporary cessation would change nothing and he said there was no need for any further contact with republicans: 'There is a joint declaration. It sets out the route, and the route is a permanent end to violence, proof that violence has ended and then a dialogue can commence. It's very welcome if people are not being mortared, killed and shot at – of course that's good news, very good news indeed, but it's not an answer.' So the government's position was clear: a permanent cessation of violence was the only key to talks.

Exactly one week before the IRA ceasefire announcement, I sat in a tiny and sparsely furnished office on the Falls Road in west Belfast and noted on slips of paper in my cheque book the latest republican briefing. The windows of the office were filled with breeze blocks, a security precaution designed to stay one step ahead of the loyalists, who not long ago had carried out a rocket attack on this building. The man I spoke to was one of republicanism's principal strategists, someone not accustomed to dealing with the press on a regular basis, and for the purpose of this conversation he was guided by a briefing note he had placed on the desk in front of him. An Irish-American delegation was due in Ireland in a couple of days' time and the inevitable ceasefire speculation had once more raised its head. The man I spoke to stressed there would be no ceasefire announcement to coincide with the visit but said there was 'no need to be pessimistic'. Republicans, he said, remained 'optimistic'. We spoke in speculative terms about how any IRA announcement might be made and he went on to tell me that what was looming 'could be the biggest story that has happened here in a quarter of a century'. He said there were no internal problems and the process remained on track. What was being hinted at here was much more than a temporary ceasefire.

The few days ahead would provide the statements from Reynolds and others that Gerry Adams referred to, the statements that would slot all the pieces of the ceasefire jigsaw into place and in those the context for the IRA cessation. I want to log much of that detail, given its relevance to what would be announced on Wednesday 31 August. That Irish-American delegation arrived in Dublin on 25 August for a meeting with Reynolds and Dick Spring; afterwards the former US congressman Bruce Morrison said that in a very frank and open discussion they had been given 'a clear understanding of the wheres and whys of [Irish] government policy at this point'. Twenty-four hours later, the same Irish-American delegation would meet with Sinn Féin leaders including Gerry Adams and Martin McGuinness at the party's Belfast headquarters at Connolly House in Andersonstown – a building that had been attacked three times by the UFF in the opening weeks of 1994. Albert Reynolds later told me they carried with them a message from his government reinforcing its demand for a complete cessation of IRA violence. 'It was delivered very clearly to the delegation when they came to see me in Dublin and they reiterated it at their meeting in Belfast and in fact they confirmed that to me after their meeting in Belfast.'

After the delegation's meeting with Sinn Féin, Bruce Morrison again spoke to the media saying his delegation had found the discussion both constructive and helpful in terms of informing them and giving them an understanding of 'where things are and where things can go'. 'We hope that the input that we have given will move that process forward. We believe that it will and we are very encouraged by what we heard here today – that the process is moving in a very constructive direction.' Later Morrison said he was hopeful of a 'dramatic breakthrough'. A key republican objective had been to internationalise the peace process they were involved in, to be able to sell their views abroad and to try to win the backing of political forces behind them. The February 1994 Adams trip to the United States had opened up that prospect, mainly thanks to the lobbying by Reynolds and Hume that guaranteed the visa, and Irish-America was making clear that more opportunities lay ahead. After the Connolly House meeting, Gerry Adams summed up his thoughts in this statement:

> We welcome the opportunity provided by today's meeting to up-date the US delegation and to give them our assessment of the present situation. The delegation similarly gave us their views of the peace process and the role they will play in moving the situation forward. In this context, I am confident that today's meeting represents an important contribution to the development of an effective peace process based on democratic principles. Sinn Féin has always recognised the importance of the international community in helping to create the conditions which can resolve this conflict. In particular, we have pointed to the positive role which Irish-America and the US Administration can play. In conjunction with the evolving peace process here, Irish-America has focused the present US Administration on the issue of peace in Ireland in an unprecedented manner and has engaged it for precisely that purpose. We welcome the role of Irish-Americans and the Clinton administration. We are optimistic that this can be built upon. Political and popular opinion in the United States can as the peace process moves forward play an increasingly central role in the search for an inclusive, negotiated and democratic settlement in Ireland. I am confident in light of today's meeting that Irish-Americans are determined to make this important contribution to the achievement of a just and lasting peace in Ireland.

On Saturday 27 August I met again the man who had been my principal republican contact throughout this whole crucial period, a man I was depending on for factual insights into republican thinking at this time. By now, I had picked up from a prison source that the ceasefire announcement could be Wednesday 31 August – certainly that was the buzz coming out of the top-security Maze jail – but the man I met on Saturday, while suggesting a decision was close, emphasised that crucial pieces of work had yet to be completed. That night I reported all of this on BBC Radio Ulster. The peace process was entering its most critical phase and statements from John Hume, Gerry Adams and Albert Reynolds would follow on Sunday, thus putting all the vital ingredients in place. Adams was now able to tell the IRA that all he had suggested was possible at around the time of Letterkenny was now in place, in fact he was able to do more than that because the IRA was able to read it for itself.

The joint Hume–Adams statement of Sunday 28 August included the following text:

We met today to review the present situation. In April last year we pointed out that everyone has a solemn duty to assist in the search for a lasting peace. Since then we have applied ourselves unremittingly to this task. As a result there has been an unprecedented focus on the development of an effective peace process. Last Easter, we indicated that we were investigating the possibility of developing an overall political strategy to establish justice and peace in Ireland. We are presently addressing this area in particular and we believe that the essential ingredients of such a strategy may now be available. A just and lasting peace in Ireland will only be achieved if it is based on democratic principles. It is clear that an internal settlement is not a solution. Both governments and all parties have already agreed that all relationships must be settled. All that has been tried before has failed to satisfactorily resolve the conflict or remove the political conditions which give rise to it. If a lasting settlement is to be found there must be fundamental and thorough-going change, based on the right of the Irish people as a whole to national self-determination. The exercise of this right is, of course, a matter for agreement between all the people of Ireland and we reiterate that such a new agreement is only viable if it enjoys the allegiance of the different traditions on this island by accommodating diversity and providing for national reconciliation. We have publicly acknowledged that the task of seeking agreement on a peaceful and democratic accord for all the people of Ireland is our primary challenge. We are convinced that significant progress has been made in developing the conditions necessary for this to occur. We underline that the process in which we are engaged offers no threat to any section of the people on this island. Our objective is agreement among our divided people. In any new situation there is a heavy onus on the British government to respond positively, both in terms of the demilitarisation of the situation and in assisting the search for an agreed Ireland by encouraging the process of national reconciliation. It is our informed opinion that the peace process remains firmly on course. We are, indeed, optimistic that the situation can be moved tangibly forward.

Things were moving quickly and a statement from the taoiseach, Albert Reynolds, would follow on the heels of that latest Hume–Adams document. Reynolds said it was clear that Sinn Féin and the IRA were in the final stages of their deliberations and he urged republicans to leave violence behind them and to make a definitive commitment to peace. He spoke of being involved in efforts to establish a viable peace process with the potential to end violence and to open up the way for inclusive negotiations leading to a just and lasting settlement. This, he said, was a historic opportunity:

Of course the British government have a heavy responsibility in all of this. They are committed under the [Downing Street] declaration to play a positive and important role in assisting the Irish people to reach an agreed accommodation for the future and in removing the injustices which have fuelled conflict in the past. In this context, I hope to see an all-round demilitarisation of the situation and the full participation of all parties, on equal terms, in talks leading to a comprehensive political settlement. It remains my view, both as taoiseach and as leader of Fianna Fáil, that in the longer term a united Ireland, achieved by agreement, offers the best and most durable basis for peace and stability. But, in any event, there can be no return to the system of majoritarian rule which caused so much abuse and bitterness in the Stormont period. Those who have been badly treated in the past need to be assured that neither selfish strategic considerations on the part of the British government nor intimidation or violence will be allowed to upset the free democratic play of forces, as they have done a number of times in the past. I am just as conscious of the fears and sensitivities of unionists, and the government fully accept the need to protect the civil and religious rights of northern unionists and Protestants and recognise that they have their own political identity and aspirations.

Reynolds said it was his judgement that the leadership of Sinn Féin was sincere in its commitment to the peace process, and he said in a new situation where violence had ceased for good he was confident that a process of inclusive negotiations, based on democratic principles, would lead to an agreed and peaceful Ireland. A decision to end violence would be a gigantic step forward in the peace process.

So, in these statements of the past few days Irish-American support for the peace process had been underscored, the taoiseach had emphasised his commitment to the achievement of a united Ireland by agreement, the issue of the need for demilitarisation going beyond an IRA cessation was pointed up in both the Reynolds and the Hume–Adams statements, and the leaders of the SDLP and Sinn Féin again ruled out any internal Northern Ireland political settlement and stressed that the Irish people as a whole had the right to self-determination, but that the exercise of that right was a matter for agreement. Sinn Féin and the SDLP still differ in their analysis on the issue of the exercise of self-determination but none the less all that was contained in these most recent statements was framed in an Irish context and it infuriated loyalists and unionists. David Ervine spoke of it in terms of pan-nationalism at its worst – not prepared to consider a unionist philosophy. The UFF said it was a recipe for civil war. In my research for this book I spoke to the DUP deputy leader, Peter Robinson, about the whole Hume–Adams process. He said there was a sense of outrage that Hume was sitting down with Adams while the IRA campaign was continuing and 'very clearly trying to form a pan-nationalist front with him'. Unionists, he said, were of the opinion that the objective was 'more to attain a nationalist goal than to achieve peace and events have shown that to be the case. The marrow of the Hume–Adams process hardened into the bones of the Downing Street Declaration and the flesh was put on in the terms of the Framework Document [a British–Irish government document agreed in February 1995].'

The final key statement before the ceasefire announcement was released by Gerry Adams on Monday 29 August; he had given the IRA leadership an updated assessment in which he expressed the belief that the current political climate provided the potential to break 'the political, constitutional and military stalemate', and the IRA for its part promised a 'speedy response'. In Dublin, Reynolds would soon be made aware of the IRA's decision. He told me he had asked through his intermediaries for some advance notice in order to be able to inform the US President and the British prime minister. Reynolds told me that John Major did not believe what he was being told and that Bill Clinton was overjoyed. For Reynolds the risks had proved worthwhile and there must have been a great sense of personal achievement. So, at the tail end of all of this to-ing and fro-ing, I met the IRA's messenger in west Belfast, a woman who carried on the tiniest piece of paper the words of that organisation's ceasefire declaration. What she read to me and what I later dictated to my news editor were words of great meaning, words that meant the possibility of something better. I reported that day that no one would dare predict that this was the end of the IRA but it was, however, the beginning of a significantly new situation.

Senior police officers at RUC headquarters in Belfast had known through their intelligence reports that the effective date of the ceasefire would be 31 August but they had not expected such a clear statement of intent from the IRA leadership. In the critical months leading to the cessation the eyes and ears of the RUC had been watching and listening as the IRA moved towards its decision. The intelligence gatherers were monitoring that intense internal debate within republicanism. Information reaching the force was obviously of good quality for a full eight weeks before the IRA's declaration of a complete cessation of military operations, the RUC Chief Constable, Sir Hugh Annesley, had told a news conference that the majority view within the republican movement was held by those who were 'genuinely looking at peace as a way forward'.

In answer to a question from me he said he had little doubt that there was a widespread debate going on within the republican movement and he believed that the issue of a ceasefire had certainly been the subject of discussion. In reply to a follow-up question from David McKittrick, the *Independent*'s Ireland correspondent, he said he suspected that both a temporary and a complete cessation of violence were being discussed. What would eventually emerge, he said, was a matter for absolute speculation.

About three months before the ceasefire announcement the intelligence services had suffered a devastating blow when ten RUC Special Branch officers were killed along with other military intelligence and MI5 personnel in a helicopter crash on the Mull of Kintyre. Among the dead was Brian Fitzsimons, the head of Special Branch and the man with primary responsibility for intelligence gathering in Northern Ireland. He was replaced in that post by one of the RUC's most experienced officers, Assistant Chief Constable Ronnie Flanagan, and as 31 August approached it was he whom the Chief Constable would have depended on for detailed briefings relating to the fine detail of that evolving republican debate. Annesley openly admits that what the IRA delivered in its ceasefire statement was more than he had thought likely or possible – indeed the categoric terminology used in respect of a complete cessation was significantly in advance of what he had expected.

Cardinal Daly also told me that he had been surprised by the 'categoric nature' of the ceasefire announcement: 'The ceasefire in many ways was surprising in its definitiveness, in its categorical character, its standing alone without apparent attached conditions in terms of time or later review or whatever. The language which was used seemed to me to indicate a conviction which was not just a passing, temporary, experimental thing but deep-going, and I felt a natural growth out of the preceding debate that had been going on.'

My conversation with the Chief Constable relating to my research for this book took place on 26 January 1995, by which stage the IRA ceasefire was almost five months old. I met Sir Hugh in his office at RUC headquarters at Brooklyn on the Knock Road in Belfast, and our conversation lasted for well over an hour. Sir Hugh's reign as Chief Constable stretches back to 1989, the same year I began to specialise in reporting the security situation for the BBC, and we had met many times both socially and in work situations. Our conversation on 26 January was over coffee. It was relaxed and on the record.

The Chief Constable told me that he believed the ceasefire decision had come from 'exhaustive meetings and discussions' and against a background of republicans being confronted by the combined might of the British and Irish governments. Sir Hugh Annesley said the IRA would also have known that security forces successes were going to get better rather than worse: 'In general terms very long internal terrorist activity does not produce results and it was never going to produce a result here of the sort that was wanted. There was no way that the British government was going to be pressed to abandon its campaign on behalf of the majority of the people on this island... there was no question of abandoning a democracy and there was a very high degree of resoluteness within the RUC and within the army that was not going to waver.' Sir Hugh said there were other contributing factors such as 'declining funds' and a concern about condemning another generation to violence. He also believes that those escalating loyalist attacks throughout the 1990s, when the UVF and the UFF first matched and then exceeded the IRA's killing rate, also had a bearing on the IRA coming to its decision. He said within some nationalist areas of Belfast people were 'progressively growing concerned' that they were at risk, that they had had enough and that there had to be a better way. 'And I think undoubtedly they were putting pressure on people primarily within Sinn Féin which was finding its way clearly back to the Provisional IRA.' He also believes the consistent condemnation of violence from within the Churches, the media, by politicians of all shades and from other community leaders had an impact. Sir Hugh said a wide combination of events had 'led to that political development and that extraordinary statement [of 31 August 1994]'. He said it was clear that the IRA could have continued to kill people and to let off bombs but that the argument within republicanism had been won by those who were saying that more could be achieved through the political route: 'Many people have said that there wasn't going to be a military victory to this campaign and I happen to support that view.'

Security sources told me that for about a month beforehand the RUC knew that the effective date of the ceasefire was going to be 31 August but they had expected the announcement to come several days earlier. These sources believe that the fact that it did not indicates that there was some 'wrangling' and 'turmoil' over the exact form of words to be used in the ceasefire statement – that right up to the last minute the IRA leadership was still considering the implications of what it was going to say. Intelligence information that there was to be a complete cessation only reached the security forces about twenty-four hours ahead of the actual ceasefire announcement itself.

The security sources whom I spoke to said the decision to opt for a ceasefire did not pass without criticism. Security sources say the main opposition to the move came from within the areas of east Tyrone and south Armagh, but when I spoke to these sources in the early part of 1995 there was no suggestion of the ceasefire being under threat. 'It's still the case that there's dissent in those areas, clearly the case that there's dissent and a high level of preparation for a return that those in those areas would see as an inevitable return.' It was stressed to me, however, that the leadership of the IRA was still very firmly in control and that there was rigid discipline. It was also suggested to me that in the run-up to the ceasefire a 'team' under the control of the former republican prisoner Bobby Storey was established to deal with dissent and to ensure that fringe groups like the Irish National Liberation Army and Republican Sinn Féin, which split from the republican movement in 1986, did nothing to jeopardise the 'peace process'.

9

WAITING FOR THE LOYALISTS

The guns of the IRA fell silent at midnight on 31 August 1994 and with the ceasefire in place Northern Ireland now waited for the decision of the loyalist leadership. The killing of the UVF and the UFF had often, and wrongly, been described as purely a reaction to the methods of the IRA: the violence that was directed against the Catholic/nationalist community had also been prompted by the fear or prospect of political change. The UFF, for instance, had often used the Hume–Adams dialogue to try to justify its violent actions and, indeed, had warned in February 1994 that it would resist with equal ferocity not only 'nationalist-inspired violence but nationalist-inspired political coercion'.

Six more violent weeks would pass before the Combined Loyalist Military Command's announcement of a universal cessation of all operational hostilities. The purpose of the CLMC since it emerged in 1991 had been to co-ordinate the loyalist response to major political developments in Northern Ireland. Alongside that command there is a Loyalist Political Alliance, initially made up of people such as Gusty Spence, David Ervine, Jim McDonald, Ray Smallwoods, David Adams and Gary McMichael, plus two 'military observers' from the UVF and the UFF – two men who in 1994 represented militant loyalism in direct and secret talks with the Church of Ireland Primate, Dr Robin Eames. That Loyalist Political Alliance has now branched out and those who belong to it have become the public faces and voices of loyalism.

There had been many significant developments within loyalism in the period stretching from the late 1980s through to 1994. Both the UVF and the UFF had raised their violent profile, and the road to the fragile peace of 1994 was littered with bodies. The mass murders – at Sean Graham's bookmaker's shop on the Ormeau Road in Belfast, at village pubs at Greysteel and Loughinisland, and at the mobile shop in Craigavon – live in the memory. So too does the UFF murder of the Belfast solicitor Pat Finucane. But the wounds inflicted by this surge in loyalist violence cut much deeper. Many families have been scarred. The main violent groups in this camp had been rearmed in the late 1980s with weapons republicans claim were supplied by British intelligence through the army agent and UDA member Brian Nelson. He was arrested, charged and convicted of loyalist terrorist offences during the Stevens investigation into collusion between elements of the security forces and loyalists – an investigation the UDA brought upon itself by showing off security force documentation that had been passed to it. While republicans talk up Nelson's role in the arms deal, loyalists have been more inclined to play it down. The period I have just mentioned also brought many changes to the UDA leadership – changes which saw younger, more militant men take over. That had a lot to do with that upsurge in violence – violence which continued right up to the point of the October 1994 loyalist ceasefire announcement. Those incidents in the first half of 1994 included a UVF attempt to bomb a Dublin pub where a republican function was being held. The bomb failed to detonate but the UVF shot dead an IRA member. The loyalist group had obtained a supply of commercial mining explosive and also used it to bomb the Sinn Féin office at Belfast City Hall.

In the weeks leading to the IRA cessation the atmosphere in Northern Ireland had once again been poisoned by violence as the people were taken on another of those roller coaster rides from hope to despair. There was at this time, of course, constant speculation pointing to behind-the-scenes developments and the probability of republicans calling a ceasefire and this was the primary reason for hope, but on the surface the cold reality of yet more killing created an altogether different mood. There was on occasions a desperate sense of hopelessness, times when people knew that the inevitable consequence of one violent action would be yet another. In those summer weeks of June, July and August loyalism suffered many wounds, including the murder of Ray Smallwoods, and in return it inflicted more hurt on the Catholic community. Political developments such as the Hume–Adams statement of 28 August, followed by comments from Albert Reynolds, also created even more suspicion and anger within loyalism, and prompted the UFF to speak in terms of civil war in the final days and hours before the IRA's announcement.

In mid-June, with the IRA ceasefire still eleven weeks away, a shooting on the Shankill Road in Belfast caused the deaths of three men and sparked a bloody and indiscriminate period of reprisal. The Shankill attack was admitted by the Irish National Liberation Army and two of the three who died, Colin Craig and Trevor King, were significant figures within the UVF. Craig died on the day of the shooting, 16 June, and King a little over three weeks later on 9 July. The Revd Roy Magee was on the Shankill Road for a meeting close to where the shootings happened. He spoke to me of an initial feeling of anger but then of overcoming that emotion and of being more determined 'to try to bring this to an end'. The minister said there was also 'a dread of retaliation; a fear of what might happen'. In this climate nothing was going to come to an end and the response of the UVF was indeed familiar and predictable.

Within a matter of hours of the Shankill attack the loyalist group shot dead a Catholic taxi driver in the early hours of 17 June. That same day bullets were fired into a workmen's hut at Newtown-abbey on the northern outskirts of Belfast. It was a random attack designed to kill Catholics but resulted in the deaths of two Protestant men. There was no statement of admission but at the time security force sources blamed the UVF. Worse was to follow: the next night the news from Northern Ireland was dominated again by yet another story of mass and indiscriminate murder. On the night of one of the Republic of Ireland's World Cup matches a pub in the tiny County Down village of Loughinisland was attacked by the UVF. Five men were killed almost instantly and a sixth died in hospital.

I was told of the shooting while I was in a restaurant having a meal with some of my family. A colleague on duty on the news desk called me twice: first, to tell me of the incident, and then to update me on the casualties. I left immediately and much of the next few days was spent in the office reporting on the incident and its implications in terms of the search for peace. At this stage the prospects were not looking good.

In an attempt to try to justify its actions the UVF had claimed that a 'republican function' had been going on in the pub but that was an allegation the security forces quickly and totally rejected. The RUC Deputy Chief Constable Blair Wallace spoke with me in his office at RUC headquarters the morning after the attack: 'These people were simply preyed upon by loyalist terrorists. The UVF, who have admitted responsibility for the incident, have endeavoured to place some respectability on their actions by suggesting that some form of republican meeting was in progress. No such meeting was taking place.' The Deputy Chief Constable said the allegation contained in the UVF statement was nothing other than an attempt to cover up 'what by any standards is an atrocity that cries out in shame'.

Wallace had been to the murder scene the night before and I asked him to describe the atmosphere and the mood.

'When I arrived in the village last night I found a sense of shock within the local community. This was the first time that their community had seen the worst excesses and the worst ravages of terrorism and really people were at a loss to know why they should be chosen for such an atrocious attack. The scene in the bar was one of complete devastation: five bodies, some lying on top of each other. It was quite obvious that the bar had been raked with gunfire and this had resulted in the deaths of those five people who remained at the scene and one who was removed and subsequently died in hospital.' Wallace said that after the violence of Thursday and Friday there was a sense that the situation would lead to 'something even more horrific' and that the RUC had been put on full alert to try to counteract the threat. Despite this heightened security, the terrorists found a way around the security cordon and attacked a vulnerable target in an isolated area.

I have found loyalists reluctant to talk about the Loughinisland incident in any detail. They won't condemn it but clearly they have difficulty in trying to justify it. It was, it seems, a kneejerk reaction to what had happened on the Shankill Road two days earlier, an incident which left loyalists concerned about the resurgence of the INLA. This was significant because later it would be a point raised by the CLMC as it considered its position in the wake of the IRA cessation.

Eleven days into July loyalism felt more pain. Ray Smallwoods, one of the principal political thinkers within the loyalist camp, was shot dead in the driveway of his Lisburn home. It could not have happened at a more emotive time on the Ulster calendar and the attack added more tension to an already volatile security situation. Smallwoods had served a prison sentence in the 1980s for his part in the attempted murder of the former MP Bernadette Devlin-McAliskey, and after his release from jail he had begun to emerge as the political face of loyalism. He gave interviews as a member of the fringe Ulster Democratic Party and as someone who had a knowledge of loyalist paramilitary thinking. At the time of his murder the IRA claimed to have shot a member of the UDA's Inner Council, but Smallwoods did not hold a position on the paramilitary leadership. He was, however, one of its key political advisers; something the UDA itself admitted in a statement following the shooting:

This morning's tragic murder of Ray Smallwoods is another example of PIRA's contribution to the peace process. Ray was a genuine and honest man dedicated to finding a just and fair solution to the present conflict. He was not a member of the Inner Council of this organisation but was one of a number of political advisers who have been actively trying to persuade the military wing of our organisation to abandon military actions. He was also involved in prison issues, himself being a former prisoner. To the Provisional IRA we say this: You talk about peace yet you murder a peace maker. It is quite clear from your actions that you wish the nationalist nightmare to continue. Direct responsibility for any actions carried out by the UFF is yours.

A flavour of Smallwoods's thinking can be gleaned from an interview I recorded with him in April 1994, a few months before his death and about a week after the IRA had announced its seventy-two-hour Easter ceasefire. He said that that ceasefire was seen within loyalism as a 'cynical propaganda ploy' – as 'another attempt to apply that bit more pressure on the British government to give that bit more to Irish nationalism'. Loyalists did not believe that what was unfolding was a peace process. It was, according to Smallwoods, 'a change in tactics' in which political violence was to be replaced by 'politically inspired coercion'. He said loyalists feared a policy of 'enforced harmonisation' taking Northern Ireland towards a united Ireland 'step by step by step'. 'Unless the integrity of Northern Ireland within the United Kingdom is recognised by nationalism – unequivocally – then there can't be peace.' Some of those words used by Smallwoods had appeared in UFF statements.

Smallwoods spoke of the type of political settlement that he believed loyalism would accept and of the relationship it would be prepared to have with the Irish Republic: 'Loyalists are ready and willing as they have been for a long, long time to put in place just and equitable institutions of government for governing Northern Ireland within the United Kingdom. When those are established and when trust is built up in Northern Ireland then we can look to ways of finding friendship with our neighbours provided our neighbours respect our constitutional integrity.'

At the time, he said, loyalists felt isolated. 'The loyalist community, I think, is angry, it's resentful and it's alienated. The loyalist people are angry at this constant pandering of the British government to Irish nationalism. For example, the Dublin government knows the British government's proposals for the future government of Northern Ireland, we don't. The people are angry with Dublin – Albert Reynolds and Dick Spring telling us that we cannot say no to all-Ireland institutions. People are angry with John Hume, who was able to make a deal with Sinn Féin/IRA but he couldn't make a deal with constitutional unionism. People are angry and they're alienated; they're alienated and let us remember that the alienation that we see now is a result of the last nationalist peace offensive, so called. In 1985 they inflicted the Anglo-Irish Agreement on us with the promise of peace, prosperity and progress. That didn't happen. What we have now is an alienation born from that, and the violence emanating from loyalist paramilitaries is the manifestation of that anger and alienation.'

Smallwoods was one of the architects of loyalist political thinking, one of its 'wordsmiths', to quote a source, and his death was a devastating blow for loyalism. He had been one of the very few from within that community prepared to articulate its views publicly and his death at the hands of the IRA may well have been intended to send a message to the loyalist terrorist leadership. The UFF had been behind that sustained series of attacks on the political representatives of republicanism and through the murder of Smallwoods the IRA was making clear that it would respond equally violently to such incidents. A loyalist source whom I spoke to during my research defined Smallwoods's role as follows: 'He would meet people we wouldn't have met and would give them our views and bring back theirs and he would advise us on what line to take. He was never privy to [Inner] Council business unless it was something we needed his advice on. The only people who had a vote on the [Inner] Council were the brigadiers and that's still the case. It hasn't changed. He was a peacemaker and they killed him at a time when he was promoting political ideas.'

The funerals of Ray Smallwoods and Trevor King both took place on Thursday 14 July. I was involved in the coverage of both, and at King's funeral on the Shankill Road I was with a BBC camera crew which had its tape taken by UVF 'marshals'. News crews were not welcome and this was being made abundantly clear. The following morning I was contacted by a loyalist source and asked to come to a location in the Woodvale area of Belfast.

Given what had happened the day before I was apprehensive but I agreed to the request and on my arrival protested at the treatment of my colleagues the previous day. It made no impact. Two of the three men who were in the room to meet me argued that republicans were using television coverage of funerals to target loyalists. They also pointed out that the media had been asked to stay away from the funeral. I listened to what they had to say but said that loyalists could not expect to dictate the news agenda. All this had nothing to do with the real purpose of my being there but it gives a flavour of the mood that prevailed at the time.

I had been asked there so that I could be given a statement from the Combined Loyalist Military Command – a statement that was intended to put further pressure on the republican movement as Sinn Féin moved towards its definitive response to the Downing Street Declaration. The loyalist terrorist leadership said that in the event of republicans ceasing hostilities it would respond to accommodate 'civilised, magnanimous and productive dialogue'. Given the hurt that loyalism had recently suffered, I was surprised by what was being said but this statement gave a rather false impression: just days later the UFF would mount an attack on another isolated pub. The text of this latest statement from the CLMC read as follows:

It is incumbent upon the CLMC to make a statement in reply to the various overtures emanating from sources whom we would hold in respect. Our ongoing campaign is not founded on the domination and privilege of one section of our citizens over the other but firmly in defence of democracy and equality and in resistance to the imposition by force of arms, coercion or persuasion of an all-Ireland republic. The prevailing nationalist nightmare is being prolonged by the wilful prevarication and unreasonable intransigence of the Provisional IRA. To date our proactive operations have been a necessary military strategy. However, the CLMC, mindful of the needs of all our people, deems it necessary to state categorically that should the republicans cease hostilities then we will respond in order to accommodate civilised, magnanimous and productive dialogue. The whole of our society must bear some portion of responsibility since all have contributed through the years by silence, word or deed. We are genuine in our intent and earnest in our quest for a peaceful solution to a conflict which has lasted centuries. Injustice and suffering are universal and no one has a monopoly on right or anguish.

I was told by the men in the room that the statement did not stand on its own but should be read in the context of the set of principles the CLMC had outlined in the period leading up to the Downing Street Declaration. In other words, loyalists would end their campaign so long as there was no weakening of Northern Ireland's position within the United Kingdom. Republicans were not impressed. Sinn Féin's Northern chairman Mitchel McLaughlin said loyalists were not serious about peace, and he went on to accuse them of being 'wedded' to failed political structures.

On the day of the statement I asked the DUP deputy leader Peter Robinson for his views on it. He thought what significance it had lay in its timing: 'I don't see anything that they haven't said before at some stage contained within the statement and therefore what significance it has, I think has probably to do with its timing and I would gauge that the message they are trying to send through that statement is one where they are putting the onus on republicans of various types. To the IRA that their violence needs to stop. To Dublin and the SDLP that their attempt to bring about a united Ireland without the democratic approval of the people has to stop, and that would be the significance I would see in it.'

That statement from the CLMC was passed to me on a Friday as the weekend was beginning and before it came to a close there was a mass murder attempt by members of one of the loyalist groups. A pub was again singled out for attack, this time at Annaclone, County Down. The incident happened on a Sunday night but the doors of the pub were closed and the gunmen were unable to get inside. Shots were fired through the windows, slightly injuring seven customers. This time, luck had prevented the security scales from being tipped once more into the area of crisis. Several days after the incident I remember asking a loyalist source to explain the attack given that statement from the CLMC just two days previously. His reply was that people were angry after the Smallwoods murder.

This was another of those dark periods in Northern Ireland during which people feared the worst, a time when there seemed no escape from that depressing climate which has so often cloaked Northern Ireland. On the final day of July the IRA shot dead two loyalists on Belfast's Ormeau Road and the pattern of events that followed was all too familiar. The men who died were Joe Bratty and Raymond Elder. Bratty was the local UDA/UFF commander, whilst Elder had been charged in 1992 in connection with the UFF murder of five Catholics at Sean Graham's bookmaker's shop in the lower Ormeau area, though the charges had later been withdrawn. The day after Bratty and Elder were murdered, just as the one o'clock news was approaching, the inevitable threat of retaliation was made by the UFF:

> Yesterday's sectarian murder of another two loyalists once again shows the hypocrisy of PIRA's peace process. We can assure PIRA that should it take a week, a month, a year, those directly involved and those who aid and abet in the murder of loyalists will be actively pursued and summarily executed.

The statement repeated what Loyalists had said on many occasions, that Elder had 'played no part' in the UFF attack on the bookmaker's shop. In the days immediately following the double murder, the UFF was involved in a series of gun attacks in the Belfast area but no one was killed.

At this time the IRA campaign was being seen as particularly provocative, including as it did that series of bombing incidents at pubs in predominantly Protestant areas; as the IRA moved towards its ceasefire it was spreading its violence across a range of targets. At the time a loyalist leadership source said it was clear that the IRA was 'prepared to sacrifice nationalist lives in retaliatory loyalist attacks'. He spoke of anger being piled on top of anger and he emphasised that even in the event of a prolonged IRA ceasefire loyalist attacks would continue.

All that was happening in this period seemed to be stoking up fear and anger within the loyalist community and it was difficult at that time to imagine that anything could be said or done to remedy what had all the appearance of a dangerous situation. Late in August the Ulster Democratic Party councillor Gary McMichael left Northern Ireland for several days having been warned that his life was in danger. He told me he had been advised by the police that there was 'an imminent threat'. Later he had learned of a republican plot to shoot him at the Admiral Benbow pub in Lisburn where he had been working part-time. The pub had been owned by his father, John McMichael, who was murdered by the IRA in 1987. A Special Branch source confirmed to me that the IRA had been targeting Gary McMichael.

The next day, Sunday 28 August, a political development occurred that infuriated loyalists. The cause of that anger was the Hume–Adams statement of that date which spoke of the need for 'fundamental and thorough-going change, based on the right of the Irish people as a whole to national self-determination'. Within twenty-four hours of the statement a scathing condemnation of it had emerged from within the ranks of loyalism. Late on Monday night I answered the phone on my desk and was asked by the caller if I would 'take a statement'. I was then given the recognised codeword of the UFF, the word used to authenticate statements when that organisation contacts the media. This was the occasion when reference was made to civil war:

> The Ulster Freedom Fighters and the Ulster Defence Association issue the following statement: Yesterday's statement by the joint chiefs of staff of the pan-Nationalist front–Hume–Adams – and its endorsement by Reynolds – does not need clarification. It is not peace that you are after but surrender. Your aggression to the loyalist people by both word and deed and your phoney so-called peace process is paramount in our thoughts at present. We care little of your speculative ceasefire talk and will not respond to it.

Rather than being, in your words, an historic opportunity for a settlement of the Ulster conflict, it is a recipe for civil war. Do you, the Irish, seriously believe we will sit back and allow ourselves to be coerced and persuaded into an all-Ireland? As we have stated before there is a price to be paid. You have not paid that price but you will. Our volunteers are well aware of the ensuing pressures we will come under. But with the support of the loyalist people and our own dedication and commitment we will overcome it for the betterment of our people and our country. For as long as 100 of us remain alive we shall never in any way submit to the rule of the Irish. For it is not for glory that we fight, nor for riches, nor for honours but for freedom alone which no good man loses but with his life.

Earlier that day in an interview with me, David Ervine of the PUP had given his response to the Hume–Adams statement; he spoke of there being anger at the 'signals' they were giving of a behind-closed-doors deal, and of there being anger at the suggestion that the essential ingredients were in place to move the peace process forward: 'What does all that mean. What does it mean when we see pan-nationalism at its worst: not prepared to consider a unionist philosophy, not prepared to consider the legitimacy of unionism and, more importantly, not prepared to accept or understand that we are British?'

Ervine said that the loyalist leaders had made it clear that they were not prepared 'to see a dilution of their nationality'. 'If their nationality is intact, therefore the partnership within the United Kingdom is intact, then I would imagine that they would be pleased to allow dialogue and accommodation.' I then asked Ervine if loyalists sensed that their nationality, that their Britishness, was under threat and his answer took just seven words to deliver: 'Very much so, very, very much so.'

That short quotation more or less summed up the mood within loyalism by the time the IRA ceasefire came into effect. It was a community filled with suspicion and with anger, and it was unsure what the future would hold. In the days ahead I would be in contact with some of the key figures within the loyalist leadership.

With the IRA ceasefire now in place, my primary task in this period was to watch for any significant movement in the loyalist camp. There would be much to-ing and fro-ing as loyalism sought clarification of the situation. Had any secret deals been done with the IRA? Was the Union safe? What will now unfold is the story of this key period; a period laced with very many important developments as loyalists edged ever closer to a ceasefire.

10
THE ROAD TO CEASEFIRE

It was Monday 5 September and with the IRA ceasefire not yet a week old speculation about an imminent loyalist response had already begun to raise its head but the situation in terms of precise thinking within the UVF and the UFF was by now somewhat confused. The previous day different signals had come through in a series of newspaper reports and late on Sunday night, as the weekend was drawing to a close, the UVF exploded a no-warning car bomb close to the Republican Press Centre in the heart of west Belfast. By teatime on Monday, however, the picture was somewhat clearer, for in the course of that day I had been in touch with two men who I knew could speak authoritatively on the UVF and the UFF. The message from both was the same: there was no prospect of an imminent ceasefire and loyalists still required clarification on several key issues. The points raised by the two men, whom I met separately, in the Shankill area of Belfast and in Lisburn, were identical. Was the IRA cessation permanent? What were the intentions of the INLA? Had any secret deal been done with republicans to secure the IRA ceasefire? And what would the Framework Document contain? This was a paper being worked on by the British and Irish governments which among other things would outline suggestions for future North–South relations. Loyalists were keen to know precisely what role was envisaged for the Dublin government in the governance of Northern Ireland.

By the time the main evening news bulletins had come round I was running reports detailing this latest thinking. Three days later the position outlined to me had crystallised into a policy statement from the Combined Loyalist Military Command. This document was passed to me when I met two men at around lunchtime on Thursday 8 September. Later that afternoon I ran reports on this latest development on BBC Radio Ulster. The statement said the loyalist leadership had been engaged in 'serious in-depth analysis' of the IRA ceasefire, and listed a series of points which the CLMC said had still to be addressed. The full statement read as follows:

> The Combined Loyalist Military Command, after serious in-depth analysis in relation to the IRA ceasefire, list below a series of points which if suitably addressed could allow the loyalist paramilitary groups to make a meaningful contribution towards peace.
>
> 1 We have yet to ascertain the bona fides of the permanence of the IRA ceasefire.
>
> 2 The intent of the INLA has yet to be established.
>
> 3 To be convinced that no secret deals have been concocted between HMG and the IRA.
>
> 4 That our constitutional position as a partner within the United Kingdom is assured.
>
> 5 To assess the implications of the joint governmental Framework Document as soon as possible.
>
> 6 It is incumbent upon the British government to ensure that there is no change or erosion within Northern Ireland to facilitate the illusion of an IRA victory. Change, if any, can only be honourable after dialogue and agreement. It is important that patience is shown to this body given the gravity of the debate required.

That evening on the BBC's national six o'clock news I was asked by Peter Sissons if any of these points raised an impossible obstacle. I said I didn't think 'impossible' and that I was beginning to believe that there were those within the loyalist camp who were perhaps just beginning to believe that no secret deals had been done with the IRA. 'They're not saying that as such but that's my hunch. On the question of whether or not the IRA ceasefire is permanent, I think loyalists accept that that is something that can be tested over a period of time and they are saying in this statement today that if they can be satisfied on these issues then it might just be possible that loyalists can make a meaningful contribution to the peace process. So I think there are some positive signals in this statement.'

The following day, 9 September, there was an important development when the Church of Ireland Primate, Dr Robin Eames, called a news conference at St Anne's Cathedral in Belfast, at which he said the prime minister had given him his word that there had been 'no secret agreement' with the IRA to bring about its ceasefire; Dr Eames added that he had been asked to make this information public. He said the loyalist paramilitaries should listen to the assurances he had been given. 'There is more to be gained in the political sense through dialogue than will ever be gained through the barrel of a gun.' This was an important intervention, for away from the glare of publicity Dr Eames had been playing a proactive role in the peace process. He was in direct contact with both governments and in recent months had held direct talks with senior figures in the Combined Loyalist Military Command (see Chapter 12). His words that day, therefore, were not only heard by loyalists but were taken on board as they continued to contemplate the future.

The following day loyalist political representatives were talking with two officials of the Northern Ireland Office at a meeting said to have been arranged through a third party. The UDP councillor Gary McMichael told me that he and the Belfast lord mayor, Alderman Hugh Smyth, a member of the PUP, attended the meeting. Significantly, this happened weeks before the loyalist ceasefire announcement and months ahead of the first round of exploratory talks between government officials and Sinn Féin. I first learned of this meeting when during my research for this book I obtained a copy of the minutes of a specially convened two-day UDP conference held at a venue in east Belfast on 13–14 September. That conference was also attended by senior figures in the leadership of the UDA. The minutes say that the meeting was requested by the NIO:

It was generally accepted that the NIO requested the meeting as a result of the CLMC statement seeking assurances on a number of points. Indeed the NIO reps. addressed each of these points in turn and our elected rep. relayed this information to us. The NIO stated their position on each of the points as follows:

1 The permanency of the IRA ceasefire was not yet accepted by the NIO and their position on it was as publicly stated.

2 The NIO had no indication of the intentions of the INLA regarding a ceasefire and wondered if that organisation were waiting to see the intentions of loyalist paramilitaries.

3 The constitutional position of Northern Ireland was not under threat and the PM gave an iron-clad guarantee that only the people of Northern Ireland could change the constitutional position.

4 There had been no secret deals done between HMG and Sinn Féin/IRA to bring about the IRA ceasefire. An NIO official pointed to the irreparable damage that such deals would cause if they ever were discovered to have taken place.

5 Our representative, on requesting to see the forthcoming 'Framework Document' on the future of Northern Ireland, at least as early as other constitutional parties, was told that this may not be possible but was left with the impression that the NIO attitude on this point may change in the event of a loyalist ceasefire.

6 Regarding concessions being presented by the IRA as a victory it was indicated that Sinn Féin, in order to appease their own supporters, are in a position of having to claim the naturally evolving changes that will be brought about by a non-violent situation as a victory.

The minutes also listed ten motions which were passed at the end of day one of the conference. The first stated: 'The UDP could not at the present time call on loyalist paramilitaries to call a ceasefire but would call for their campaign to be streamlined.' It was also decided that the UDP would seek permission for a delegation to hold talks at the top-security Maze jail with representatives of the 'loyalist prisoners of war'. Requests were channelled through the Prison Service and the Political Affairs Department at the NIO, but before such a meeting could come about the prime minister, John Major, visited Belfast on 16 September.

Speaking at Stormont, he promised a referendum on the outcome of the political talks process, a commitment which he said meant that no one could go behind the backs of the people of Northern Ireland. 'You can forget this talk of secret deals. It will be for you to decide,' he said. The prime minister said he was looking for a clearer indication that the IRA's campaign was over for good but he emphasised that it was not their violence alone that had 'scarred the life of Northern Ireland'. He said loyalists should end their campaign and he added that there was not a shred of justification for it continuing. 'The loyalists should make good their earlier statements that their violence would end when IRA violence was halted. They should now respond to the many appeals to them from political, church and community leaders.'

There was a sense now that the promise of a referendum, alongside the assurances that no secret deals had been done with the IRA, would secure a ceasefire: loyalists were beginning to believe that the Union was safe. But before any decision would be taken, the UDA leadership was insisting that it would first have to consult with its prisoners. The breakthrough finally came on Monday 10 October.

That day I was at home on leave, but I wanted to keep tabs on the situation and made a routine call to a loyalist contact. This call proved valuable. I learned that two meetings had taken place that day at the Maze prison, important meetings which had been specially arranged for a day on which the jail was not usually open to visitors. In the first meeting a PUP delegation had met UVF inmates, and in the second members of the UDP had held talks with UDA–UFF prisoners. The two outside delegations had included some of the most influential figures in the loyalist paramilitary camp, among them the UVF leader and four members of the UDA's so-called Inner Council.

The Revd Roy Magee had been involved in the process of

trying to arrange the talks, and my next call was to him. Reluctantly he confirmed the information I had and agreed that he would do a short interview with one of my colleagues. First, however, he wanted to inform one of his contacts at the NIO that the story of the meetings was about to break. From home I briefed my friend and colleague Mervyn Jess and it was he who put the information to the NIO. The government confirmed the meetings and said they had been allowed so as not to place any obstacle in the way of a potential loyalist ceasefire. At 9 p.m. the BBC broke the story on its local and national outlets.

These meetings were not of crucial importance to the UVF; it had already completed an extensive consultation process within its ranks, a process in which its prisoners had been fully briefed in a series of jail visits. The UDA, however, had not reached this point and members of its leadership were stressing that no decision on a ceasefire could come ahead of Maze talks. So the meeting at the Maze was a crucial part of the UDA's consultation process. Seven prisoners – four of them sentenced and three on remand – took part in the discussions. They were influential voices within the loyalist structure – three had previously held positions on the UDA Inner Council. Four current members of that leadership – the UDA's so-called 'brigadiers' in east and west Belfast and in south-east Antrim and north Antrim/Londonderry – were on the outside delegation, which was completed by John White, a former life sentence prisoner who in the weeks and months following this meeting would become one of the public faces of the emerging UDP.

In a typed message to the UDA leadership on the outside, the prisoners advised that a continuation of a military campaign could prove 'counterproductive', even 'detrimental' to the loyalist cause. The full text of the statement read as follows:

> We the UDA/UFF volunteers after much discussion have come to the conclusion that to continue our military campaign under the present circumstances could be counterproductive and in the long

term detrimental to our cause. We appreciate the difficulties in targeting known republicans with the increased security in loyalist areas. We acknowledge the unacceptability of targeting non-combative nationalists. In the present political climate a ceasefire by loyalist volunteers would be seen by our long-suffering community as a contributing factor in establishing a lasting peace within Northern Ireland. In the event of a loyalist ceasefire we feel the maintenance of our command structure and the retention of war materials for the defence of the loyalist people is essential. Should republicans renege on their peace commitment and return to their genocide against the loyalist people we would fully support our command structure in returning to reactive/proactive measures against the pan-nationalist front. We the UDA/UFF LPOW [loyalist prisoners of war], Maze, feel we must be seen to be giving this fragile peace process every opportunity to succeed and that our per-manent cessation of violence should last as long as the republican complete cessation of violence.

The statement was dated 10 October 1994 and was said to come from all UDA/UFF prisoners of war.

The following morning I interviewed John White, who said that, in terms of movement towards a loyalist ceasefire, another obstacle had been overcome. I asked why he thought the NIO had allowed the meetings to take place and he said they would have known 'quite well' that 'an agreement could not be reached unless dialogue was opened up with the prisoners'. The same day, the minister for political development at Stormont, Michael Ancram, spoke of a one-off decision by the secretary of state to allow the talks: 'He [Sir Patrick Mayhew] didn't want to put obstacles in the way of a dialogue which might lead to a cessation of violence on the so-called loyalist side as well.'

During my research for this book, I learned that within hours of the Maze meeting the UDA leadership met at Rathcoole on the northern outskirts of Belfast. The meeting brought together the organisation's six so-called 'brigadiers' – the four who had been part of the Maze talks plus the group's leaders in north and south Belfast. Agreement was reached on a ceasefire and two days later,

121

on Wednesday 12 October, the leaders of the UDA/UFF, the UVF and the Red Hand Commando met in the Shankill area under the umbrella of the Combined Loyalist Military Command and agreed the wording of the announcement of a cessation of violence.

At 9.30 that night, I sat in an office in the Woodvale area of Belfast after being contacted and asked to go there along with another Belfast journalist, Ivan Little of Ulster Television. We were met by several senior loyalist figures and were left in no doubt that a ceasefire announcement was imminent. The former UVF leader Gusty Spence, who had been jailed on a murder charge in the 1960s, handed us a sheet of paper giving details of what was termed 'an unprecedented press conference' to be held the following morning. The news conference would be jointly hosted by the Ulster Democratic and Progressive Unionist parties.

When I left the building I immediately called my news editor Tom Kelly and dictated several sentences over the phone which, shortly after ten o'clock, were used in a BBC Radio Ulster news flash. The loyalist ceasefire announcement was now precisely eleven hours away.

11

THE UNION IS SAFE

The IRA had used a clandestine meeting to announce its 'complete cessation of military operations'. Loyalism chose an entirely different means of spreading the news of its ceasefire. On 13 October 1994 it put a panel of its 'political' people before the media; on this historic day loyalism was taking a giant step out of the shadows. Those in front of the cameras, David Adams, David Ervine, Gary McMichael, William Smith, Gusty Spence, John White and Jim McDonald, were people known to me. Most, but not all of them, had spent years in jail and here they were in 1994 sending out a message of peace. At last, after twenty-five years of killing, Northern Ireland could begin to look to a better future.

It took exactly forty-three days for the loyalist terrorist leadership to respond in kind to the IRA cessation. In that long and uncertain six-week period a young Catholic man, John O'Hanlon, was shot dead by the UFF. There were several other murder bids including failed attempts by the UVF to kill the leader of the Irish National Liberation Army and a Sinn Féin councillor. That same loyalist group was also behind several explosions including the car bomb attack close to the Republican Press Centre. In another incident a device which had been concealed on the Belfast–Dublin train partially detonated as it pulled into Connolly Station in the Irish capital. The UVF was playing a high-risk game with no-warning bombs, which could so easily have claimed more lives. There was an attempt, too, by the UFF to attack customers in a north Belfast pub, but the gunmen failed to get inside the bar. But even as the violence continued, despite the uncertainty there was a sense too that the loyalist groups would eventually have to bring a halt to their campaigns: the question really centred on how long it would take.

Not long after the republican ceasefire announcement graffiti accepting 'THE UNCONDITIONAL SURRENDER OF THE IRA' appeared in loyalist parts of Belfast, but the reality was altogether different from the writing on the walls. It took those six weeks leading to 13 October for the CLMC to put its name to a statement proclaiming the Union between Northern Ireland and the rest of the United Kingdom to be safe.

At 7 a.m. on Thursday 13 October the BBC Radio Ulster news bulletin led with a report suggesting that a loyalist ceasefire announcement was expected later that morning. Immediately after the news, on *Good Morning Ulster*, I was asked by Barry Cowan what was known of loyalist intentions.

I said it was likely that the ceasefire announcement would contain some conditions. 'Within a week of the IRA ceasefire announcement the loyalist terrorist leadership outlined its terms for a similar gesture. At that time it said it would need to know if the IRA ceasefire was permanent and it also wanted a declaration of intent from the INLA. Now that declaration hasn't come. Republicans haven't used the word "permanent" and one assumes at this stage that loyalists will announce a ceasefire saying that their guns will remain silent so long as that remains the case on the republican side.'

I was then asked if we could be reassured that loyalists were speaking with the one voice.

'Absolutely. Any decision within loyalism to call a ceasefire would have to be ratified by this so-called Combined Loyalist Military Command which has control over all the violent loyalist groupings – the UVF, the UDA and the Red Hand Commando – and it's understood that that loyalist terrorist leadership met yesterday in Belfast and finalised its response to the IRA ceasefire and to the current political situation.'

In the course of the interview I pointed out that loyalists had

124

not yet said how they would want to be represented in any future talks but I mentioned the fact that the Progressive Unionist and Ulster Democratic parties had recently taken on a much more prominent public profile and suggested that the loyalist paramilitaries might well believe that their views could be represented by those parties. By 15 December, nine weeks into the loyalist ceasefire and on the first anniversary of the Downing Street Declaration, delegations from the PUP and the UDP began exploratory talks with government officials at Parliament Buildings, Stormont.

The ceasefire announcement was made at Fernhill House, a community centre on the Glencairn estate, just after 9 a.m. The seven representatives of the PUP and UDP took their seats and faced the media in a packed room. These, we were told, were the persuaders, men whose 'political analysis' had helped coax the paramilitaries to this point; huddled at the back of the room, out of view of the cameras, were key figures among the persuaded – members of the loyalist terrorist leadership who the previous day had sanctioned the statement now about to be read. First, however, there was an opening statement from Gary McMichael in which he spoke of Northern Ireland being on the verge of a new beginning: 'If we are to find a true and lasting peace in our country we must share the responsibility of the past and lead the challenge of the future. If we are to have any hope of establishing a lasting peace we must recognise and respect the diversity of the two traditions in any future structures, finding peace through consent. Today represents the first tentative steps towards a new and better Northern Ireland – a land that is fit for its people.'

It was then the turn of Gusty Spence to speak – and deliver the words of a supplied statement from the CLMC. In a moment of drama he removed a sheet of paper from an envelope and declared: 'This is the instrument, this is the article.' I remember thinking, what a contrast between now and what had happened six weeks previously. The IRA declaration had been delivered in a whisper – no cameras, no microphones, no questions, no fuss – while here

125

the CLMC had opted for all the attention of the media. The statement first gave the background to the ceasefire decision:

> After a widespread consultative process initiated by representations from the Ulster Democratic and Progressive Unionist parties, and after having received confirmation and guarantees in relation to Northern Ireland's constitutional position within the United Kingdom, as well as other assurances, and, in the belief that the democratically expressed wishes of the greater number of people in Northern Ireland will be respected and upheld, the CLMC will universally cease all operational hostilities as from 12 midnight on Thursday the 13th October 1994.

Then came the conditions the CLMC had attached to the cessation:

> The permanence of *our* ceasefire will be completely dependent upon the continued cessation of all nationalist/republican violence. The sole responsibility for a return to war lies with them.

There then followed a tribute to those who had been involved in the violent loyalist campaign:

> In the genuine hope that this peace will be permanent, we take the opportunity to pay homage to all our Fighters, Commandos and Volunteers who have paid the supreme sacrifice. They did not die in vain. THE UNION IS SAFE.
>
> To our physically and mentally wounded who have served Ulster so unselfishly, we wish a speedy recovery, and to the relatives of these men and women we pledge our continued moral and practical support.
>
> To our prisoners who have undergone so much deprivation and degradation with great courage and forbearance, we solemnly promise to leave no stone unturned to secure their freedom.
>
> To our serving officers, NCOs and personnel we extend our eternal gratitude for their obedience to orders, for their ingenuity, resilience and good humour in the most trying of circumstances, and we commend them for their courageous fortitude and unshakable faith over the long years of armed confrontation.

In the lead-up to their ceasefire decision, loyalists had raised questions about the permanence of the IRA ceasefire, about the intentions of the INLA and about the future status of the Union. Now, in bold print, the CLMC was stating its view that the constitutional position of Northern Ireland was safe. Though loyalist and republican political objectives remained as far apart as ever, the CLMC was saying that so long as the cessation of republican violence continued, the guns of the UVF, the UFF and the Red Hand Commando would be silent.

The statement also carried these words of remorse:

> In all sincerity we offer to the loved ones of all innocent victims over the past twenty-five years abject and true remorse. No words of ours will compensate for the intolerable suffering they have undergone during the conflict.
>
> Let us firmly resolve to respect our differing views of freedom, culture and aspiration and never again permit our political circumstances to degenerate into bloody warfare.
>
> We are on the threshold of a new and exciting beginning with our battles in the future being political battles, fought on the side of honesty, decency and democracy against the negativity of mistrust, misunderstanding and malevolence, so that, together, we can bring forth a wholesome society in which our children, and their children, will know the meaning of true peace.

When Gusty Spence had finished reading the statement, I asked him what he considered to be the one key factor that had taken the loyalist paramilitaries to their ceasefire position. His answer was straightforward: 'Force of argument put forward by the Ulster Democratic Party and the Progressive Unionist Party that the violence had to come to an end. We had to give peace a chance. The prime minister had given undertakings – firm undertakings – that Ulster's position within the United Kingdom would be safe, and I think that had a big bearing on the Combined Loyalist Military Command coming to their decision.'

Looking to the future, David Ervine said that no section of the community should be excluded from talks on the future of Northern Ireland. He added that it was very important that the loyalist paramilitaries be given 'some vent to an expression'. The message was clear: loyalism was emerging from its backroom closet and wanted a place at the political talks table. This in itself was significant: less than a year earlier David Ervine had given his first television interview – to Ulster Television – in silhouette, his identity concealed from the viewer. In fact, for years loyalist spokesmen had shied away from cameras but now there was a whole new confident mood.

The ceasefire announcement was welcomed by both the British and the Irish prime ministers. John Major spoke of another very important part of the jigsaw falling into place. 'What we now need to do is to absorb what has happened, consider it and then decide how to move forward. We'll do that in our own time and in our own way but I'm delighted with the news we have heard this morning.' In Dublin, Albert Reynolds said the decision of the loyalist leadership effectively signified 'the end of twenty-five years of violence and the closure of a tragic chapter in our history'. The SDLP leader John Hume spoke of a 'great day for the people of Northern Ireland' but a day also to remember all of those who had died and their families.

The leader of the DUP, the Revd Ian Paisley, posed questions about the assurances loyalists said they had been given. He asked who had given these assurances and how valuable they were. Leading republican Martin McGuinness spoke in terms of a new beginning. He said the situation was very encouraging and very heartening and had opened up all sorts of possibilities, but he restated his view that there could be no internal political settlement within the six counties. The Alliance Party leader Dr John Alderdice said the day's developments heralded 'a whole new series of opportunities', adding, 'We cannot now afford a vacuum that would allow this tremendous opportunity to unravel.' There were words of warning too from the Church of Ireland Primate, Dr Robin Eames, who begged governments and politicians to 'make the most of this opportunity'.

12

IN GOD'S NAME STOP

In mid-November 1994, I sat across the table from Dr Eames at his office in Armagh. Through a number of sources I had learned of his efforts to help develop the peace process and of his direct contacts with members of the loyalist leadership. In turn he had been told by the Revd Roy Magee that I had begun to write this book: the archbishop had then asked me to arrange a meeting.

The talks between representatives of the Combined Loyalist Military Command and Dr Eames had been set up by the Revd Roy Magee, who himself had played an important role in persuading loyalists to end their violence. His contacts with the paramilitary leaderships became a matter of public knowledge in 1992 when he arranged a meeting between two former Presbyterian moderators and the UDA's Inner Council. Those talks broke down when Dr Jack Weir and Dr Godfrey Brown also opened discussions with senior figures in the Sinn Féin leadership including Gerry Adams. A leader of the UDA told me at the time: 'Our door is open to anybody and everybody but at the end of the day we could not talk to anybody who was going to have discussions with Provisional Sinn Féin.'

The door did, however, remain open to Dr Magee, who had no role in the Sinn Féin talks. In the months ahead the minister would find that others were keen to hear his views and to include him in their company. In the periods leading to the Downing Street Declaration and to the IRA ceasefire he was in direct contact with the Irish government and had several meetings with the then taoiseach, Albert Reynolds, in his Dublin office. He also told me of contacts with British officials at Stormont. Dr Magee said his purpose in talking to Reynolds was to advise him of the concerns within the Protestant community and to emphasise that there were two sides to the equation: 'that unless loyalists stopped, the war wasn't over'. He said he also made the point that there should never be a deal done in exchange for an IRA ceasefire and that any constitutional change should require the support of a majority of the Northern Ireland community.

Dr Magee told me that on 29 August 1994 Reynolds called him at his Dundonald home to advise him of the possibility of an imminent IRA ceasefire statement. He said the taoiseach said that there would be 'no halfway house': the ceasefire would be permanent. Reynolds emphasised that no deal had been done: the situation was as before and 'the consent of the people of Northern Ireland would be required before any change in the constitutional position'.

Dr Magee told me he then relayed the news to the two main loyalist paramilitary groups. He contacted a member of the UDA's Inner Council in south-east Antrim and a man close to the UVF leadership. All of this may explain how the Combined Loyalist Military Command was in a position to give its initial reaction to the IRA ceasefire before the actual announcement.

This type of contact between Dr Magee and the loyalist leadership happened regularly, and as far as the churchman was concerned had the principal purpose of trying to influence an end to violence. It was in that context that Dr Eames agreed to direct talks with representatives of loyalism.

Unlike Dr Magee, Dr Eames carries the responsibility of leading a major church. He has been Church of Ireland Primate for around ten years, and his position has gained him access to the highest political offices in both Britain and Ireland. In the run-up to the Downing Street Declaration he entered those offices to inform the British and Irish prime ministers of the concerns of the Protestant community and to advise them on the type of language that could prove acceptable to a majority of people in Northern Ireland. On occasions his advice was given in the form of a written submission.

Driving the archbishop was the desire to see an end to the type of killing that had plagued both communities in Northern Ireland for twenty-five years. He had buried many victims of violence and he told me he had become convinced that some sort of Church intervention was necessary. But he was also aware that he should take personal responsibility for so doing even though he felt a majority of people would support him.

The role that Dr Eames played in the peace process has by and large gone untold, but when I met him a month after the loyalist ceasefire part of his story at least had begun to unfold. We agreed that our conversation would be on the record (which may have restricted more of the facts from coming out). What now follows is the account Dr Eames gave me of his involvement with the two governments and of his direct talks with loyalists.

'When it became clear that they [the two governments] were leading up to what was then to become the Downing Street Declaration I began to get very worried because I believed that unless there was a direct input to Dublin on what was concerning the Protestant people of Northern Ireland, and given in a way which hadn't just a party political label, that agreement could do a great deal of damage and make the situation worse.'

It was a time when fears that the situation would worsen haunted the church leader. He spoke of a perception within the Unionist–Protestant community that 'the sell-out' had begun. At the time unionist politicians had access to the British government but they were not talking to Dublin and this in part prompted his intervention.

'To me, if Dublin were to use language that would be totally unacceptable to Protestants in the North we would be in an extremely difficult situation. Therefore I welcomed the opportunity given to me to discuss the fears of the Protestant people in Northern Ireland directly with the taoiseach. That discussion centred on such things as the need to have the consent of the majority to any change in the constitutional status of Northern Ireland.' Dr Eames said he was also making Reynolds aware that 'there were inherent suspicions among Protestants in Northern Ireland of what were the aims of this forthcoming joint declaration'. He said he felt he had a clear duty to answer specific questions put to him by the taoiseach and that in several meetings he put to Reynolds what he thought would possibly be 'the bottom line to make sure that Protestants did not feel that this was a sell-out'.

Throughout the discussions in London and Dublin Dr Eames emphasised that he was not a party politician and that his involvement in these talks stemmed from his responsibilities as a church leader who had seen so much suffering in Northern Ireland. He spoke of a desperate burden in his mind and heart and of a fear that unless something was done to move the situation in Northern Ireland forward, the prospect of civil war was a reality.

Much of what the archbishop had to say to Reynolds was also repeated in talks with the British prime minister. 'It was obvious to me that it would be totally wrong to speak entirely to the taoiseach and therefore I welcomed the opportunity given to me of accepting an invitation to talk to the British prime minister about the fears in this community and at that stage I was able to tell him again of what I was perceiving to be the genuine Protestant fears in Northern Ireland. But I was also able to say to him that I could sense what were the reasons for the fears in the Roman Catholic population. It was as balanced an approach as I could make to him.'

As things developed, Dr Eames said he got the impression that both prime ministers took his input seriously, and he came to the opinion that he was not wasting his time. He was looking for an even-handed approach from the two governments. He wanted the joint declaration to contain something that would push the situation forward, 'that would allow pressure to be brought on the paramilitaries to stop', and he said he felt it important that the people of Northern Ireland should feel that they were not being dictated to over their own heads. He told me that he was 'encouraged' when the declaration eventually emerged ten days before Christmas 1993. That sense of being encouraged came from the fact that the absolute principle of consent was enshrined in the document: that constitutional change could only come about if a majority in Northern Ireland so desired.

It was in the months after the declaration that Dr Eames agreed to meet with representatives of loyalism: not, he said, to act as a negotiator or a go-between carrying messages to the two governments but to tell them directly that in God's name the killing must stop – they must try to find that politics and political involvement was the way forward. He said he was introduced to some people by Roy Magee. 'I didn't know what their allegiance was or anything else but he assured me that it was important that they heard what I had to say. At no time did I seek any identification of those I met, just the assurance that they had some influence.'

The archbishop said he had been told that the men had 'considerable influence within the loyalist paramilitary community'. 'I was not prepared to talk to those who wanted to engage in an academic discussion. I wanted people who would hear why I condemned them, why in a Christian sense I believed what they were doing was wrong, and why I believed I had to urge them to seek another way of making their voice heard.' The two men whom Dr Eames met on several occasions were representatives of the CLMC: one a member of the UDA Inner Council and the other a senior figure in the UVF leadership.

As our conversation progressed I asked the archbishop why he had chosen to speak directly to these men.

'Everybody was going public in condemning them – politicians, churchmen, overseas, everybody was condemning them. They were issuing statements justifying what they were doing, making excuses and I wasn't wearing it. To me it was morally wrong to kill a Catholic. It was morally wrong to bomb a pub. It was morally wrong to kill any human being and I said to them at one stage, I believe that there would be more than enough justification for you not even waiting for the Provisional IRA to cease – for you to stop and to allow the welling up of relief in this community that you had stopped to make even greater pressure on the Provisional IRA to stop and thereby create a situation in which talking could begin.' Dr Eames said the talks had provided him with the opportunity to tell the men face to face and not through public statements that violence was taking them nowhere.

Before meeting the archbishop, I had learned from a number of sources that he had been given a position paper by the representatives of the CLMC, and this was something he confirmed when we spoke: 'They asked me if I would look at something, a document showing what their concerns were. I read the document and I said to them, I'm not a negotiator but nevertheless, as the British government has said it will not negotiate with Sinn Féin, I couldn't see that there would be negotiations on these, but I would have thought that in a ceasefire situation most of these could be addressed, but addressed in a dialogue situation, not down the barrel of a gun.' Dr Eames said the document reinforced his belief 'that there were enough within the loyalist paramilitary camp thinking along lines of dialogue – there was sufficient thinking that was taking them beyond blind violence.' The archbishop took on board the points that had been made in the statement, and in his continuing conversations with politicians, he told me, he was able to say to them, 'You know the sort of thinking that I believe lies behind this violence is as follows and I said these are the sort of things I would hope would be addressed in a ceasefire situation.'

A little over seven weeks after I had spoken to the archbishop, I obtained details of the document he had been given by the CLMC. I was told that it had first emerged within loyalism in March 1994; its text shows that the loyalist paramilitary groups were seriously contemplating a ceasefire long before the IRA's August announcement. The statement, passed also to the Revd Roy Magee, read as follows:

> Despite propaganda to the contrary, anyone with a discerning interest in the security affairs of Northern Ireland will note that the loyalist paramilitaries have observed an appreciable amount of restraint in their ongoing campaign. The security forces and only they have been instrumental in thwarting our attempts to strike at

our primary targets. There is genuinely no desire on our part to confront or engage the forces of our country in which many of us have served with distinction. Being mindful of what is called the peace process, the CLMC wishes to offer to their government terms for consideration which would enable hostilities from this source to cease. The two sovereign governments will then be free to apply their negotiative skills if the declaration [the Downing Street Declaration] is accepted by the Provisionals or their considerable forces against them if it is rejected.

1 The setting up of incident centres within the CLMC areas of influence to monitor the ongoing security situation.

2 In order to foster trust there would be no retrospective loyalist arrests.

3 No house searches in the absence of loyalist military activity.

4 Reasonable and liberal access to prison population under CLMC influence to persuade and explain.

5 Responsible and rational negotiations relating to the loyalist prisoners in the enhancement of the release scheme.

6 Protection for at-risk CLMC personnel in the event of almost certain PIRA provocation.

There is ample precedent for the six points which we have made, the most recent of which was the governmental arrangement with the Official IRA when they decided to call an indefinite ceasefire. We are concerned that positive political progress should be made so long as the rights of the majority of the people of Northern Ireland are upheld by HMG and an honourable accommodation arrived at with our minority population and their representatives. Believe us when we state that these terms are not made from a position of weakness, as your intelligence services will no doubt confirm. We too have come a long way in the political thought process.

With their offer of terms for a ceasefire, loyalists were trying to outmanoeuvre the IRA and put more pressure on the republican movement as a whole, but when those IRA attacks in June and July claimed the lives of prominent loyalists the prospect of the CLMC bringing a halt to its violent campaign ahead of an IRA cessation of military operations had gone. 'We couldn't have called a ceasefire then. In the eyes of the loyalist community we would just have been lying down.' Those words were spoken by one of the CLMC representatives involved in the contacts with Dr Eames. 'People in the loyalist community were expecting something to happen in response to the Smallwoods and Bratty murders. The intention at that stage would have been to hit at somebody senior in the republican movement, but that was a virtual impossibility.' According to the source, loyalists were prevented from carrying through their plans because their areas had been swamped by the security forces. Nevertheless, loyalist violence continued through the summer and autumn.

The moments of hope for Dr Eames that had been produced by the secret March 1994 statement that had suggested that a loyalist ceasefire was possible were followed by times of absolute despair; none more so than in the immediate aftermath of the Loughin-island pub shootings. The archbishop sensed then that his approaches were being ignored; he was aghast and horrified by what had happened, and through Dr Magee he sent a message to loyalists telling them that he believed they had turned their backs on his pleas for them to stop. Dr Magee remembers that Dr Eames posed the question to him: 'Are we wasting our time?' Dr Magee too was disgusted by what had happened in Loughinisland, but he said he had been assured that what people were seeing 'was not a true reflection of the direction in which loyalists were moving at that time'. Archbishop Eames told me that after the Loughinisland inci-dent he had very little contact with the loyalist paramilitaries, but he did intervene again in a less direct sense when loyalists started to seek assurances that no deals had been done to bring about the IRA ceasefire. He said that as Primate of All-Ireland and as a churchman he put a categorical question to the prime minister on the matter. 'He said to me – the words exactly – you have my solemn oath that nothing has been done behind the scenes to bring about the Provisional IRA ceasefire.' Dr Eames said he had asked Major if he could make this information public and was told that he could. The news conference at St Anne's Cathedral followed (see page 117) at which he begged the loyalist paramilitaries to accept the assurance he had been given.

I asked Dr Eames if his news conference was specifically designed to transmit a message into the loyalist camp.

'I was doing this because I was not prepared after Loughinisland to say that I had any further role in talking directly to them, but I still felt in my heart that this statement would do something to bring them to their final decision. I had no way of knowing if they would listen. I'd no way of knowing if they were hearing, but I had reason to believe that they wanted that sort of an assurance given.'

Loyalists were indeed listening, and were taking seriously what the archbishop had to say. 'He was a man of his word and we took him as a man of his word,' one of the loyalists involved told me. 'We were of the view that John Major wouldn't lie to him. We then had to make a decision, do we accept it [the assurance of no secret deal with the IRA] or not? And in the end we accepted it.' The source said the assurance given by Dr Eames and the prime minister's promise of a referendum were two of the key factors that helped bring about the loyalist ceasefire. A senior figure in the UVF leadership also spoke of the archbishop being an important piece of the jigsaw. Ahead of the ceasefire announcement Dr Eames was given an indication of the wording that was to be used. He told me his reaction was one of sheer prayer and personal relief: 'I thanked God particularly because I had said to them at one stage, you know a ceasefire is going to be very, very hollow unless you can say something about the victims of violence, and I was relieved when I saw they spoke about remorse. I realised also that there'd be mixed feelings in the public mind about this, but I was relieved and it meant that maybe some of the things I'd said had been listened to, but I've got to emphasise to you my overall feeling, when I heard what they were going to do in a matter of days, was to thank God and to say to myself the worry and the strain and the risk – your words – had in fact perhaps been justified.' Dr Magee also experienced a tremendous feeling of relief at hearing the ceasefire announcement. After the Greysteel shooting, it seemed as if his public appeal for no retaliation in the wake of the Shankill bombing had been ignored, and for a while he felt like walking away from his contacts with the loyalist leadership. It was a gut reaction, which stemmed from frustration and a feeling that there was nothing more he could do, but he did not give in to it; he continued to make his appeals for an end to violence.

When I spoke to Albert Reynolds in his office at Leinster House in Dublin on 2 February 1995 he used the words 'hugely important' to describe the roles played by Dr Eames and Dr Magee. In his period as taoiseach Reynolds had established a network of contacts in Northern Ireland's Protestant community. He said he was conscious of the need for an even-handed approach and of the need to address the parallel fears running through the communities. The views being put by Dr Eames and Dr Magee meant that Reynolds was being made aware in a very direct sense of the concerns within the unionist/loyalist community. Magee, he said, had played an 'invaluable role'.

Dr Magee told me that at one stage he made Reynolds aware of conversations he was having with loyalist paramilitaries about a bill of rights. Indeed in October 1993 Dr Magee told me of a document he was discussing with the leaderships of the UDA and the UVF, a document which in six short sentences recognised a number of rights, including the right of free political thought, the right to seek constitutional change by peaceful and legitimate means, and the right to pursue in a democratic manner national and political aspirations. The wording of this document found its way into the Downing Street Declaration a little over two months later, having been placed there at the request of Albert Reynolds.

The former taoiseach told me: 'When the Downing Street Declaration came out for the first time the people on the loyalist paramilitary side saw that people were listening to them and that Roy Magee was not just wasting his time talking to them; that he could demonstrate that people were listening and that they were listening at the highest levels of government on both sides. And I think Archbishop Eames, having entrée to my office and having entrée to Number Ten Downing Street, left him in a very key position as well.'

After the ceasefire announcement, Dr Eames told me his role was to encourage people to start thinking of what the ingredients of peace would be. A mountain had been climbed, but he feared that in the euphoria of the occasion complacency could cause a vacuum. 'The biggest mountain to climb was to build and hold the peace.' There was a need, he said, to take seriously and to engage politically the representatives of those who had previously been involved in violence, and he felt the voices emerging from within the loyalist community should be heard.

13

MEN WITH NO MANDATE

Those voices that Dr Eames referred to were beginning to be recognised by the Northern Ireland public, particularly those of David Ervine and Gary McMichael. I can remember the first interview I did with Ervine in January 1994 for a *Spotlight* documentary on loyalism. He was nervous, keen to know the questions and, given the sensitivities attached to the period, he was answering from a prepared script. Months later he had become an altogether more confident performer; by now there had been chat show appearances, numerous newspaper interviews, and regular outings on television and radio. The media wanted to know more about this man and where he was coming from. Ervine talks of loyalism having a 'great message' but fears the prison background of many of its spokesmen could forever prove damaging in terms of trying to win a popular electoral mandate. In the pages that follow I speak to some of the emerging loyalist voices and to the man believed to have been the principal author of the loyalist ceasefire statement.

In terms of electoral support the Ulster Democratic and Progressive Unionist parties hardly register on the political map – both have the tiniest of mandates – but their importance in relation to the peace process stems from the fact that on 13 October the Combined Loyalist Military Command opted to give politics a chance and agreed that its views could be represented in any talks forum by the UDP and the PUP.

Outside their own community the two parties were hardly known before the ceasefire and few would have had a knowledge of what they stood for. The UDP has its roots in the paramilitary

UDA while the PUP has a relationship with the UVF. This was something I asked to be defined when I spoke at length with Billy Hutchinson and David Ervine of the PUP over lunch in a club in the back streets of the Shankill area of Belfast about one hundred days into the loyalist ceasefire. The conversation was on the record, and the two men spoke in the direction of the small tape recorder I had placed on the table. In the background the daily routine of the club continued as normal. There was the sound of the fruit machine being played in the hall, above the bar the television was tuned to BBC 1 for the one o'clock news and for the Australian soap *Neighbours*, and the women behind the bar served out the lunchtime specials of pork and steak. Those in the club would occasionally glance towards the corner where I sat with the two loyalist representatives, men whose faces were becoming more familiar in Northern Ireland's changing situation. It was Billy Hutchinson, a former life sentence prisoner (who was to lead the PUP into exploratory talks with government officials nine weeks into the cessation) who took my question on the links between the PUP and the UVF: 'The relationship is a very strict one in terms of acting as political confidants and providing political analysis for them, but it doesn't go any deeper than that.' Both men said the Progressive Unionist Party did not believe in violence and had never acted as apologists for it. But, I asked, did that mean they condemned it? Again the answer came from Billy Hutchinson: 'Obviously if we want to try to influence people who are carrying out acts of violence there is no point in condemning them. It's about understanding why they do it and then trying to convince them that political dialogue is the way forward.'

David Ervine also is a former prisoner and is arguably the most articulate spokesman to have come out of the ranks of loyalism. He believes that on both sides of Northern Ireland's religious divide there is a need to lay to rest many ghosts and many myths. For its part, Ervine says, loyalism is prepared to acknowledge the tragedies of the past. 'When I was a boy the great saying was "We are the people". For 1994 most unionists would settle for being a people and gone is the sense of jingoism and triumphalism. I think tragically we are faced in some respects with a reversed triumphalism – a reversed jingoism which nationalism has to deal with. We need to calm the rhetoric on both sides and stop the absolutist language which in a divided society is the creation of further division – a perpetuation, if you like, of "them and us" and therefore the perpetuation of conflict and unless we move away from that the abyss will always be looming for this society.'

Ervine speaks of his party trying to create an 'honest, reasonable, living peace within Northern Ireland', but he accepts that it may well have difficulties in gaining an electoral mandate given the prison background of many of its members. 'It's rather a Catch-22 situation. We believe that we have a great message but perhaps we are bad messengers.' His hope is that the changing situation will also change voting trends and attitudes and in turn provide his party with a real mandate. 'People are fickle and we have to leave that to their discretion. Certainly we will attempt to achieve one [a mandate] although that's not simply what we are about. We are about trying to create a lasting peace. It's country before party and I think we have said that on more occasions than one. We do infer, of course, that there are those who put party before country and indeed self before country, but that's a matter for them and how they are interpreted by the people.'

Billy Hutchinson speaks in terms of conflict transformation rather than conflict resolution – basically because he believes the diverse positions of nationalism and unionism cannot be reconciled. The best hope for Northern Ireland, he believes, is that its violent battle can be transformed into a political battle. All of this would mean influential people on both sides of the religious divide working in a number of spheres, including within the paramilitaries, to achieve an acceptable interim deal. At this point in our conversation Ervine interjected to say that Northern Ireland needed to escape from the tragic scenario of winners and losers. Everyone had been a loser in the quality and style of life that had existed there throughout the twenty-five years of the Troubles;

the challenge now was to create winners in a more pragmatic and realistic fashion – 'a fashion which elevates the life and the value of life and the quality of life for all of the people.'

'Them–and–us societies operate very much from the perception that "they do better than I do" and I think we have to try to create the checks and balances in this society to ensure that if anybody does better than anybody else it is not because there is an unequal opportunity.'

Within the fringe loyalist groupings there is a sense of having been let down, of having been failed by the two traditional unionist parties. Gary McMichael of the UDP speaks of trying to offer an alternative voice. He told me a situation had been allowed to develop in which the two main unionist parties had been the only players, but he spoke of politics changing, of loyalism being given a clear platform in the wake of the ceasefire and of its voice at last being heard. McMichael, who was his party's only elected representative at the time of the ceasefire, believes that in time the party may obtain an electoral mandate, although he does not expect any substantial improvement in the UDP's electoral performance in the short term. 'I know we have got widespread support within the loyalist community for what we are doing. That support has always been there but has never emerged electorally. Our views – the political principles that we advocate – have been stifled because we were in a violent situation . . . and it's only when you take the violence away that people within the loyalist community are able to open their minds to allow themselves to manoeuvre politically.' He suggested the politics of loyalism had failed to make an electoral impact because of the negativity attached to the 'base politics of fear and mistrust'.

McMichael's party colleague, David Adams, knows the reality of trying to win votes for the loyalist position. At the polls, votes for loyalist candidates have tended by and large to amount to hundreds rather than thousands; indeed, when David Adams contested a local government election in Lisburn in 1993 his tally of first-preference votes was 283.

'Against a backdrop of violence, ordinary people found it very hard to accept that the Ulster Democratic Party were serious about their proposals within a document, say, like *Commonsense*, whereas now that there is no backdrop of violence people see that we are entirely serious about that and they are starting to take us seriously and our political proposals seriously.' Weeks into the ceasefire, however, there was still no sign of the electorate warming to the UDP. The party contested a by-election for a seat on Newtown-abbey district council but failed to make an impression. In a field of five, its candidate Tommy Kirkham finished back in fourth place, well behind the candidates from the two main unionist parties.

The *Commonsense* document David Adams referred to was first published by the UDA at the beginning of 1987. It proposed a Northern Ireland Assembly and Executive to be elected by pro-portional representation, a bill of rights, and a written constitution; much of the UDP's current policy is based on this document.

David Adams was part of the UDP/PUP team that announced the ceasefire. He then travelled to the United States with several others to put across the loyalist message, and when exploratory talks began with government officials at Stormont in December 1994 he was part of his party's delegation. When I spoke to him the ceasefire was into its fourteenth week and his mood, I suppose, could have been summed up as upbeat but cautious. He believed it would take time to heal the many wounds inflicted during the Troubles. 'For the past twenty-five years it was very, very easy to retreat back into your own tribe or your own camp and sit and shout the old slogans and blind yourself to realities. I very much feel as if we are taking the first tentative steps out into no-man's-land as it were, and it will be a slow process.'

He spoke of political accommodation within an internal Nor-thern Ireland frame and said the water was continually being mud-died and clouded by talk of external relationships. The primary relationship that had to be addressed as far as he was concerned was the relationship between the people who live in Northern Ireland – 'the two warring factions'.

'The people here won't give their consent to influence in the internal affairs of Northern Ireland by an outside force, but the thing is, anybody with any sense wants to have a friendly relationship with their neighbour but things have to be taken in the right order. We have to build a relationship with the people who live closest to us. In our case, us being Protestants, that is with Roman Catholics. We have to build a relationship with them.' He said the onus was very much on unionists to prove to the nationalist people that the likes of the old Stormont regime will never be allowed to exist again: 'The onus is very much on us to prove to our nationalist neighbours that their best future, their safest future, and their rights will be enshrined properly within a Northern Ireland framework.'

McMichael picked up on this point. He remains bitter about his father's murder but believes the time has come to leave the past behind. 'You've got to decide when enough is enough and you can't have your emotions ruled by history and the history of your experiences. You've got to try to rise above it and decide what is right and what is good and I think that's what we are trying to do. The governments, the political parties, all have a responsibility to persuade others that their view is right. That's what politics is all about. It's up to unionists to persuade nationalists that they can play a full and equal role in society – that they have nothing to fear from a Northern Ireland within the United Kingdom. It's up to nationalists to persuade unionists if they have an aspiration towards a united Ireland that they are not going to coerce the political situation to develop that aspiration.' Ideally, McMichael said, a framework should be built within which the two communities in Northern Ireland could play a full role without fear or mistrust of the political process itself.

Gary McMichael, David Adams, Billy Hutchinson and David Ervine have given a new voice to loyalism, but the security forces believe that a veteran loyalist was the principal author of the ceasefire statement – its flowery language points to the hand of Gusty Spence. He was undoubtedly one of the main persuaders in

145

the background dealing that went on prior to the ceasefire announcement, and a little over three months later, on 26 January 1995, I chatted with him for about an hour at his home in the Shankill area of Belfast. It was a conversation that dealt with many issues including the state of the Union, the ceasefire statement and its words of remorse, the loyalist philosophy, the past and, more important, the path ahead.

Spence believes the coming together of loyalism under the umbrella of the Combined Loyalist Military Command to have been highly significant. Although the violent loyalist groups kept their 'operational' autonomy, they spoke with the one voice when it came to major policy decisions. The first time they did so under the label of the CLMC was in 1991, when in the days leading to the Brooke talks at Stormont they announced their conditional ceasefire. According to Spence the opportunity had presented itself 'for the loyalist paramilitaries and to some degree the loyalist political confidants to express their bona fides and their genuine interest in peace'.

'It was a big breakthrough. It was the first taste of universal ceasefire from a loyalist perspective. Unfortunately there was no reciprocation on the IRA side. As a matter of fact there was an intensification in order to provoke; to ensure that the ceasefire broke down. It didn't break down despite the severe provocation. It held until it became obvious that there was going to be no form of political rapprochement in the immediate future in relation to the Brooke talks. So as a result of that the Combined Loyalist Military Command called off the ceasefire and things moved into maybe a more vicious stage.'

Spence hopes that this time, with the IRA also in the frame, more political progress can be made. 'First and foremost we have to recognise our diversity. We have to accommodate that diversity. It's only whenever diversity is used in provocative terms that it becomes a problem. It must not be used to provoke. It must not be used to divide. Whenever we sit down we have to understand that the destiny of our society depends on us. The peace of our society and our children and their children depends on us.'

Spence, like David Adams, speaks of the need to reach an accommodation, of a need to recognise the rights of people to differ politically and of a philosophy which embraces humanity, decency and caring. I found it difficult to take on board these words, words that were being spoken by a man who had spent long years in jail having been convicted of murder, but the situation in Northern Ireland is changing and Spence says it must be recognised that people too can change. He does not believe that the positions of unionism and nationalism or loyalism and republicanism can be reconciled, but he says that if the guns are silent and if the political forum is where the battle is taking place, so be it. For Spence, unionism is a legitimate 'national statement', but he believes that within that unionism working-class politics has been stifled. New voices are emerging, however, and he believes it is vital that they are heard. He speaks of people having come out of their trenches – out into the open – and he says it is important now that the political realities of Northern Ireland are recognised: 'Until such times as the greater number of people want things to change then things will remain as they are. Once we recognise that, all things are possible.'

The rock on which the loyalist ceasefire was built was the assumption that the union with Britain was safe. Spence is convinced that it is and has a list of reasons for saying so.

'Unionism has always suffered from the jitters. They've always – despite the bombasting, despite the bellicose statements from time to time – they have been absolutely insecure because they have never ever realised their strength. The Union is safe because a million people say that it is safe. The Union is safe because the British government – despite what people say about the British government's word – the British government, the Irish government and indeed the American government say that the Union is safe. It's safe through the Downing Street Declaration. It's safe through the continuous and strenuous promises that the British government have given.' He also believes that republicans have accepted that the British presence in Northern Ireland consists of the one million Protestant/unionist/loyalist people. 'So how do they deal with them? Do they kill them all? Do they achieve their all-Ireland and expect the Prods to come to heel? It doesn't work that way.'

I then asked Gusty Spence whether the words of remorse written into the loyalist ceasefire statement amounted to an acknowledgement that the killing of the previous twenty-five years had been wrong. His answer was not given in black-and-white terms. 'From a personal point of view I wasn't speaking about twenty-five years. I was speaking about every injustice that had been perpetrated by Protestant on Catholic or Catholic on Protestant or government on people. That's what I was speaking about. I was speaking about all time.'

Spence believes that the future will provide loyalism with an electoral mandate and he suggests that not only will the loyalist political groups 'catch up' on Sinn Féin but that they might even move ahead. Given the fact that the combined UDP/PUP vote in the last local government elections amounted to less than one per cent, the analysis seems ludicrous, but it is nevertheless Spence's view.

When I left his home I travelled across Belfast to its east side for a lunch appointment with the deputy leader of the DUP Peter Robinson MP. We discussed his assessment of the ceasefires, how 'safe' he believed the Union to be, and how he thought the PUP and the UDP would perform in future elections.

On this point he recounted a conversation he once had with the late John McMichael of the UDA. 'He had carried out a count of all the members of his organisation in the constituency in which he stood – I think it was for the Assembly – and worked out that they had about 1,500 members and joyfully concluded that each would have a family perhaps of three voters and therefore he would have something in the region of four to five thousand votes which would be the sort of base that would be necessary to win the seat. I think he ended up with about six hundred votes or thereabouts which showed that even his own membership hadn't been prepared to come out to the ballot box. So I think you cannot assume people to have a mandate or that their views are going to be acceptable to the electorate and that's something that nobody can predict. That's what democracy is all about. It's up to them [the UDP and PUP] to seek a mandate and to see if they receive it.'

I asked Robinson if the two traditional unionist parties feared in any sense the emerging voice of the UDP and PUP. His answer was no. 'We haven't felt any impact by the creation of these two parties. There were always people within our party whom we recognised, or believed perhaps, had a closer association with one of these two smaller parties. To some extent it clears the lines when they have gone over to those parties but it wasn't anything on the scale that the press were predicting.' Weeks after the loyalist ceasefire announcement three DUP members – including two councillors – moved to the Ulster Democratic Party. One of the three was Tommy Kirkham, who subsequently failed to win the Newtownabbey by-election.

On the issue of the ceasefires, Peter Robinson expressed the view that the IRA cessation was purely tactical – that it had been delivered in the hope of winning more concessions from the British government – and he disagreed with the loyalist analysis that the Union was 'safe'. Unionism, he believed, remained under threat.

'The principle of the IRA ceasefire wasn't based upon the IRA believing that what it had been doing was wrong and should come to an end. It was a tactical decision – that they would cease their violence in the belief that they might be able to wring further concessions from the government by ceasing violence than by continuing it. Therefore it was a ceasefire which was conditional upon them receiving concessions and that is the position at the moment. If the government gives the concessions then the IRA ceasefire will be maintained. If they don't, then the IRA will go back to violence and that means that the pressure is on the government to pay a further-stage payment to keep the IRA quiet and that gun is always held to the head of the government.'

Peter Robinson spoke of a constant battle for unionism because nationalists had never accepted the state of Northern Ireland. He said no unionist 'with hand on heart' could say there was no foreseeable danger to the Union. Given this context he said loyalists were faced with two choices: they could either tell the people they got it wrong or 'worse than that they attempt to tell the people that all of the changes that take place are not endangering the Union and that effectively puts them on the side of the government for any future change.' Robinson said loyalists had judged the situation badly – they had been wrong to indicate that the Union was safe when 'manifestly it was not'. He said it would have been wiser for the loyalist leadership to have said there were advantages for the unionist community in a total cessation of violence 'and we are prepared to pursue our campaign in a political direction'. 'That would have been the best option. That would have brought an end to violence. It wouldn't have committed themselves, if you like, to dependence on any future British government. But I think they are in the worst of all worlds because they are now in the position where they either go along with whatever a British government does or they have to stand up and say, We got it wrong.'

Weeks into the loyalist ceasefire there were some voices within that community querying the analysis that the Union was safe. Alec Kerr is not one of the public faces of loyalism but at one time he was one of its most influential figures. He was on the loyalist remand wings of the Maze prison facing charges at the time of the ceasefire announcement and soon afterwards was given bail. Weeks later, as 1994 was drawing to a close, I interviewed him for the BBC Radio Ulster *Seven Days* programme. He spoke as a member of the UDP but his influence within loyalism at that time was believed to stretch far beyond that party. In the interview he said people were 'beginning to show concern' over the possibility that the Union was not as safe as had been made out. He said the concern stemmed from the constant talk about cross-border bodies or institutions. Such bodies would operate within an all-Ireland infrastructure and would, he feared, give an even greater Irish dimension to the internal government of Northern Ireland. He said the peace process seemed to be bowing to Sinn Féin's every whim and if the trend continued there would be problems. 'The next few months will be a very testing time for the peace process.'

14

TALKING AT STORMONT

In December 1994 the men who have emerged as the political representatives of loyalism, many of whom know the meaning of life on a prison wing, walked in the corridors of power at Stormont as the government opened exploratory talks with the UDP and PUP. These were part of a wider talks process designed to take Northern Ireland beyond the point of two ceasefires and closer to a real peace settlement. For the government team, the principal issue for discussion in these talks was that relating to the decommissioning of the illegal weapons still held in loyalist arms dumps across Northern Ireland, while the UDP and the PUP wanted to ensure that their voices would be heard in the political debate on Northern Ireland's future. All this represented something new for the inexperienced loyalist team, but confidential minutes will show they were quick to argue their case when it was suggested that they would have only a limited role in the envisaged political talks process.

For the political representatives of loyalism the talking at Stormont began on 15 December 1994, on the first anniversary of the Downing Street Declaration and nine weeks into the loyalist ceasefire. The UDP and PUP were each represented by five-member delegations, led respectively by Councillor Gary McMichael and Billy Hutchinson. Those they met were senior government officials led by an English civil servant. This delegation also included a former Controller of Prisons in Northern Ireland, a man who now holds a senior position within the NIO department that deals with security policy. The government's position as it entered this exploratory dialogue was outlined in a thirty-six-paragraph opening statement. The loyalist delegations were told that the government's priority in Northern Ireland was to achieve 'peace, stability, reconciliation and prosperity' for all the people of Northern Ireland, and 'to establish locally accountable democratic institutions carrying widespread support and acceptance within a wider framework of harmonious relations based on consent'.

The government's statement was read by the English civil servant. The ten loyalists in the room heard him say that for twenty-five years all sections of the community had endured 'violence and immeasurable human suffering'. The community had 'overwhelmingly rejected' that violence and had 'supported the principles of democracy and consent, as set out in the Downing Street Declaration'. Paragraphs 3 and 4 of the government statement then said:

> That declaration offered a framework for a better future and set out a clear path by which the Progressive Unionist Party (PUP) and the Ulster Democratic Party (UDP), and others, could come to play a full part in democratic life. There had first to be an assurance that violence was at an end. The statement by the Combined Loyalist Military Command (CLMC) on 13th October, as progressively confirmed in subsequent actions, has made it possible for the government to open this exploratory dialogue now as the next step in the process.
>
> It is through this dialogue that peace can be consolidated and loyalist political representatives can demonstrate their commitment to exclusively peaceful methods and the democratic process, and so take the opportunity offered by the Downing Street Declaration to enter as fully into normal political life as is consistent with their electoral mandates. It is therefore of critical importance. Senior government officials, acting under ministerial direction, are entering these exploratory discussions with the utmost seriousness and in a positive spirit with a commitment to bringing them, if possible, to a successful and satisfactory conclusion.

All these points were made in the introduction section of the government's document, a paper which then went on to explain the basis of exploratory dialogue:

The government is entering this exploratory dialogue with the following purposes:

- to exchange views on how the PUP and UDP would be able over a period to play the same part as the current constitutional parties in the public life of Northern Ireland; and
- to examine the practical consequences of the ending of violence.

As the British and Irish governments reiterated in the Downing Street Declaration, the achievement of peace must involve a permanent end to the use of, or support for, paramilitary violence. The continuation and completion of this dialogue depends on the CLMC's continued adherence to this in word and action regardless of other circumstances and on loyalist political representatives demonstrating a commitment to exclusively peaceful methods and showing that they abide by the democratic process. One of the clearest demonstrations of adherence to these principles will be the safe removal and disposal of illegally held weapons and explosives. Also important will be clarification of the PUP's and UDP's attitude to the use of violence in any circumstances, and of their relationship to the CLMC.

Paragraphs 26 and 27 of the government document dealing with 'The Talks Process' caused the ten loyalists in the room some considerable concern. Because of their tiny electoral mandates neither the PUP nor the UDP would have a formal role in any inclusive talks process involving the two governments and the major political parties. The two paragraphs read thus:

It remains the government's belief that all the most fundamental issues facing Northern Ireland can be most satisfactorily addressed and resolved through inclusive political negotiations addressing a broad agenda across all the relevant relationships with no issue excluded and no outcome predetermined. Participation in such a talks process, involving the two governments and other political parties, is open (as paragraph 10 of the Downing Street Declaration makes clear) to 'democratically mandated parties which establish a commitment to exclusively peaceful methods and which have shown that they abide by the democratic process'. Neither the PUP nor the UDP currently command a sufficient electoral mandate across Northern Ireland, comparable to that of the other political parties already involved in the talks process, to secure formal participation in such a talks process. However, the government would want to keep the PUP and the UDP, along with other parties who had demonstrated a commitment to exclusively peaceful methods but were not formally involved in the talks process, in touch at the appropriate level with its general thinking and in broad terms with the development of political dialogue, and to take account of their views.

Exploratory dialogue cannot anticipate any part of the negotiations that constitute the talks process. But, with a view to exploring how the PUP and UDP might come to be kept in touch in broad terms with and contribute to the development of political dialogue through the talks process, the government believes it would be helpful to set out its approach to the talks process.

The government document then set about explaining its approach to the talks process, the aim of which, it said, was to achieve a 'stable, durable and workable political settlement' which could secure 'widespread consent across the community in Northern Ireland'. The document gave the background to the process and set out the steps that lay ahead, which would include the publication of the 'Joint Framework Document' being worked on by the two governments. (This document was eventually published by the two governments on Wednesday 22 February 1995 – and prompted a hostile unionist response. The governments were accused of operating to a nationalist agenda.)

When the English civil servant had finished reading the government's statement, Gary McMichael read the UDP's opening statement. He said that that day represented 'an historic step towards a resolution of the conflict in Northern Ireland'. The party's statement said everyone must enter the process with courage and imagination: 'It is incumbent on all parties to play a full and constructive role in the pursuit of peace. Whatever our aspirations for the future, whatever our backgrounds, no one has the right to deny our people, especially our children, the best possible life chances. The Ulster Democratic Party [enters] these preliminary discussions in a confident and realistic manner, with the interests of Northern Ireland and its people first and foremost in our mind. We recognise the difficulties which lie ahead. Nothing can be guaranteed. Creating the peace has been difficult – cementing that peace will prove infinitely more challenging. But a basis for agreement must be reached. This may be the last opportunity to build a peaceful society together. We must co-determine the future of Northern Ireland, building accountable, democratic structures based upon respect and equality of citizenship. The scars inflicted from centuries of distrust and twenty-five years of conflict will not disappear overnight. It would be naïve to believe otherwise, but we look forward to a future where there are no victims of conflict and political prisoners form part of a distant memory.'

The UDP document then set out some of its proposals for future government in Northern Ireland. It called for an elected assembly saying 'the political vacuum which perpetuates instability must be filled with democratic and accountable structures'. Proposals from the UDP also called on the government to establish a commission to formulate a bill of rights for all the citizens of Northern Ireland. The UDP said unionism had 'a responsibility' to convince nationalists that their best future was within 'a new and progressive Northern Ireland where no one is denied their rights or aspirations'. The final part of the UDP statement read as follows:

Twenty-five years of conflict has resulted in widespread social and economic deprivation within working-class areas in both communities. Economic regeneration is an essential component of conflict resolution and social reconstruction. It is important that a structured programme be engaged which can demonstrate accountability and parity of investment. Regardless of supplementary investment from whatever source, the British government must make a firm, long-term commitment to at least maintain its current level of subvention to Northern Ireland. There must be an equal commitment from all sides to the 'normalisation' of society. In order to redress the abnormalities which have been created by twenty-five years of conflict and political instability, we must aid the transition from war to peace by addressing issues such as policing in the community and the removal of special legislation. Of vital importance is the release of political prisoners and their reintegration into society.

It was then the turn of Billy Hutchinson to present the opening statement from the PUP. The party outlined its position in a four-page document broken down into eight areas. Section 1 read as follows:

Although it has been often stated that the constitutional position of Northern Ireland is secure, it should be clear to all that the indigenous British population have some serious misgivings in relation to proposed cross-border institutions. Those fears are real and should be addressed as soon as is practicably possible by the government. The Framework Document – the basis of 'strands 2 and 3'; the suggestions for relationships between the peoples and governments within the British Isles – should reflect the will of the greater number of people within Northern Ireland. We echo the sentiment of the Queen's Speech: 'The future of Northern Ireland will be founded in democracy and consent.' It has been pleasing to hear that consent is to be the predominant factor and that imposition has no part in our future. This is a realistic approach. Put simply, without the consent of the greater number of people any initiative is doomed to failure. That is the right of the people.

The theme of conflict transformation was woven into the PUP document:

There is little hope, at least in the short term, of resolving the conflict. The implacable opposites of nationalism and unionism are irreconcilable. However, we believe that movement by all to the legitimate political arena can create the transformation from armed conflict to dialogue.

The document also touched on the issues of prisoners and weapons. The PUP said it would be taking on a 'proactive role' in seeking to convince the government of the need to regard 'the release of political prisoners as being integral to the peace process'.

As for the decommissioning of weapons, the party said this was an issue that would take time to resolve:

> The issue of illegal arms in our society cannot and will not be dismissed lightly. Ideally we wish that none existed at all. Alas, we are all too well aware that this is not the case because of the distrust which exists. The formula necessary to create disarmament will indeed be hard to find. We are committed to the search for that formula. As with all who address the contentious issues which so beset us, we too are bound by the realms of possibility. Hence, we fear that the resolution of this issue is some way down the road.

In its opening presentation the PUP also focused on the issues of unemployment and the need for economic regeneration. It summed up by saying that it recognised the difficulties along the road in the transition to the democratic process.

Gary McMichael told me during my research for this book that after the opening statements had been completed, discussion on paragraphs 26 and 27 of the government document took up most of the subsequent conversation. Loyalists were not amused by the idea that they would be locked outside the talks process proper, and the leader of the UDP delegation argued that their relevance to the talks 'could not be judged solely on an electoral mandate'. A text of confidential minutes of this meeting obtained during my research read as follows:

> The UDP criticised the government's opening statement for appearing to suggest that their and the PUP's involvement in the political process could only be limited. It was wrong to focus solely on electoral support to determine the level of participation, since parties such as the UDP had a latent mandate stemming from their position within the community and the role they had played in building peace. They should not suffer the penalty of restricted access to the political process because they had succeeded (not without risk) in brokering the CLMC ceasefire. The PUP said that the two parties' role should not be limited to the single issue of arms, as the statement in places appeared to suggest. They had a wide agenda and a mandate which could not simply be measured

in terms of votes. On the arms issue, the two parties had to work at building up the trust in their community which would be necessary to enable progress to be made in this area. The government said that the fact that full-scale exploratory dialogue was being held with the two parties showed that the government fully acknowledged the position of the PUP and UDP in the political and community life of the province. The issues to be addressed certainly went wider than arms, but the fact that the loyalist paramilitaries retained the capability to resume their activities, and that the two parties clearly had a substantial insight into and influence with the paramilitaries (as the ceasefire statement itself indicated) meant that progress in the exploratory dialogue was a necessary preliminary to a fuller political role for the two parties.

This text was drawn from a set of agreed minutes and it shows the depth of concern expressed by the two fringe parties. Neither was prepared to accept a bit-part role in the talks process. Both, from the outset, despite their tiny electoral mandates, were demanding a place on the bigger stage if and when the talks reached that point. The newest players on Northern Ireland's political field were pointing up their part in brokering the peace and demanding their say in any negotiations on the future.

The day after that first exploratory meeting, I interviewed the former UDA leader Andy Tyrie in the UDP's Shankill Road office. It was the first television interview he had given since 1988 – the year he was ousted from the Inner Council of the UDA. I had asked for the interview some weeks earlier after learning that Tyrie's advice had been sought in the run-up to the loyalist ceasefire. He was being consulted by a member of the UDA leadership and also attended the UDP conference in east Belfast the month before the ceasefire was announced. At that conference he stressed the importance of the UDP getting its message across in the United States and said the party must work at building an electoral mandate. When I interviewed him on 16 December he said no one should be excluded from the talks process: 'We have a situation here where we have government ministers coming over here and they have not been elected by the people of Northern Ireland

and they are representing – they are talking for us – and they have been doing it for quite a number of years and they haven't been doing a very good job of it and I would rather see some of our people [UDP members] that have not been elected speaking for us because they know what it's about.' The former UDA leader said that Gerry Adams had 'lost the war' and was now trying 'to win the peace'. He said the clear message that should go out was that there was a peace for everyone to win and it should be won together.

When I spoke to him he said he believed the loyalist ceasefire was solid, though the loyalist paramilitaries were 'capable of moving back into violence'. 'There's no desire to do it at this moment in time but I think if it is necessary they will do it. But they have never applied a threat during the whole period of time of the ceasefire and they have no intentions of doing it. They have said: "We have handed over to a different department. We support our political representatives. We are going to give them all the help we possibly can."'

As for the decommissioning of weapons – the principal issue raised by the government team in that first exploratory talks meeting – there was no sign of any early breakthrough. Indeed, on 24 January 1995 the CLMC released a statement saying that the arms issue could not be addressed until such times as there was 'trust' in the political process and until it reached the point where a settlement was in sight. The statement was passed to me and Ivan Little of Ulster Television during a meeting in the Shankill area. The CLMC was responding to unionist expressions of concern about how the political process was developing. By this stage, there had been a great deal of speculation about the pending publication of the Joint Framework Document and what it might contain in terms of proposed cross-border bodies. The loyalist terrorist leadership said it recognised the 'fears and apprehension' within its community relating to that speculation. It reiterated its commitment to the six principles it had outlined in its December 1993 policy statement and said it believed that these could 'create the conditions for a just and equitable settlement within Northern Ireland'. The loyalist leadership again stressed that a Northern Ireland Assembly at Stormont must decide on any cross-border relationship. So, while the political representatives of loyalism continued to talk at Stormont, behind the scenes the leaders of the UVF and UFF were still expressing deep concern about the process aimed at taking the situation in Northern Ireland into the area of a permanent peace. More trust, more persuasion and more talking would be needed before that goal could come closer to being achieved.

15

A PERMANENT PEACE?

No one can tell what the future holds, but already huge progress has been made in Northern Ireland. At the time of writing the two ceasefires have already outstretched most people's expectations, and the hope is that the peace can now become permanent. Things that were totally unthinkable a year ago are now taken for granted. Around 1,000 soldiers have returned home to Britain, police officers walk the streets without army cover, and politicians have been meeting to discuss issues of common interest. It is part of a process designed at building up trust in a place where there are still deep suspicions. In an interview with me in April 1995, senior RUC officer Ronnie Flanagan, a man tipped as a possible future Chief Constable, said he believed the peace could become permanent. He did make the subtle distinction between *could* and *would* and pointed out that there were still difficult balances to be found and difficult paths to be trodden, but he was optimistic and he is a man well placed to weigh up the situation here. Those difficult balances will have to be found by the politicians. The challenge for those in government, people such as John Major, Sir Patrick Mayhew, Michael Ancram, John Bruton and Dick Spring and whoever else might come along, is to find a way of gently coaxing this process along and keeping everyone on board. There have been angry voices but the guns have been silent.

The seven-strong leadership of the IRA, its so-called Army Council, can 'declare war' or 'conclude peace' but the latter requires the approval of an IRA 'army convention', a specially convened meeting representative of the entire organisation. No such convention was held in the run-up to the 31 August 1994 ceasefire announcement and at the time of writing (June 1995) it still had not happened – in other words the IRA has not yet decided that its 'peace' is to be permanent. This is an issue the British government and unionists focused on in the immediate period following the ceasefire announcement. John Major said he was greatly encouraged by the IRA's statement but said clarification was needed if this was indeed intended to be a permanent renunciation of violence. Similar words came from the Northern Ireland secretary of state, Sir Patrick Mayhew, who said it needed to be made clear that violence 'was over permanently – that is to say for good'.

That clarification of the terms of the IRA ceasefire came from the organisation after another 'blunder' – in the wake of a disastrous setback for Northern Ireland's developing 'peace' situation. On 10 November 1994 a postal worker, Frank Kerr, was shot dead during a robbery in Newry in which £131,000 was stolen. Immediately, a suspecting finger was pointed at the IRA in south Armagh; indeed on 11 November when I spoke to a security source I was told that this incident went to the heart of that organisation. It transpired that this was in fact an IRA robbery, not sanctioned by the overall leadership but carried out locally. 'Condolences' were offered to the Kerr family and the IRA explained that its ceasefire banned all use of arms. The Irish government demonstrated its disapproval by reversing a decision to grant early releases to a number of IRA prisoners being held in jails in the republic, but those releases have since gone ahead and indeed have been followed by others.

Many other significant political and security developments flowed from Northern Ireland's new situation. Albert Reynolds held to his pre-ceasefire pledge and met Gerry Adams publicly along with John Hume within a week of the IRA's cessation of military operations. For this Dublin meeting the Sinn Féin president was accompanied by Jim Gibney and the party's director of publicity, Rita O'Hare: two more key figures in the ranks of republicanism. Sinn Féin would later take its place in a Forum for Peace and Reconciliation established by the Dublin government.

In its first session the forum included addresses by the taoiseach, Albert Reynolds, the Irish foreign minister, Dick Spring, the main opposition leader in the Republic, John Bruton, John Hume, Gerry Adams, and the Alliance leader John Alderdice. The Sinn Féin delegation included two more of the party's senior figures, vice-president Pat Doherty and general secretary Lucilita Breathnach, who was also part of the Sinn Féin team which began exploratory talks with British government officials in December 1994. These talks followed a government 'working assumption' that the IRA ceasefire was intended to be permanent. But in the early months of 1995 those talks became bogged down in a wrangle over the decommissioning of IRA weapons and stalled progress towards Sinn Féin engaging in talks with a British minister. A path for these talks was finally cleared in late April when the government decided it would introduce the political development minister, Michael Ancram, into the discussions. Republicans, however, were still not happy with the way things were developing at this point. They complained that their electoral mandate was not being recognised and demanded to move beyond exploratory talks and into the wider process. In contrast, the Dublin government at its most senior level was engaging republicans in dialogue; following the fall of Albert Reynolds there were direct talks between the new taoiseach, John Bruton, and Gerry Adams. These talks also involved Dick Spring. In another development, in March 1995, on his third visit to the United States, Adams met the American President Bill Clinton; during this latest visit the Sinn Féin president was permitted to fundraise on behalf of his party, a decision that infuriated John Major. A visit by Major to Derry in May was disrupted by a Sinn Féin protest in which clashes developed between republicans and the police. Major said this justified his government's cautious approach in terms of talking to Sinn Féin and he said if that party wanted to be part of the democratic process then its members and supporters should behave like democrats.

In other security developments in the post-ceasefire period troops were taken off the streets and some were withdrawn from

Northern Ireland. Border roads were reopened, but when I spoke to him in March 1995, Gerry Adams was still of the view that Britain had not fully engaged in the 'peace process', a process he said was still not irreversible.

'What is now an opportunity, it's now a cliché, the best opportunity in seventy-five years – no one knows – me, you, Dublin, London, no one knows how it's going to turn out. No one can call it, and what of course is clear is that if we don't remove the causes of conflict we will indeed not only have squandered the best opportunity for seventy-five years but the causes of conflict will nurture, will fester and will resurrect. And when I say things like that – and I refrain from saying it, because it's taken as a threat – it isn't a threat, it's a statement of fact.'

Much of this book has focused on the vital roles of John Hume, Gerry Adams, Albert Reynolds and Irish-America in terms of bringing about the ceasefire, but there was another vital player in the field, a churchman who has stayed away from publicity but who played a crucial part in this peace process. Gerry Adams did not name him when we spoke but I knew who he was talking about: 'We would not, and I've said this about John Hume, but we would not have even the possibility of a peace process if it wasn't for the unstinting, patient, diligent work of a third party. There is no doubt that he was the constant in all of this and in the development of relationships between the key players. He was the key to it and he brought a very special quality to it.'

The man that Gerry Adams refers to as 'a third party' is Father Alex Reid, a priest at the Clonard monastery in west Belfast whose picture was carried in many newspapers in March 1988 – a picture which showed him praying over the body of an army corporal who was one of two soldiers killed after being abducted at an IRA funeral. This all happened in a mad week in Northern Ireland which included a loyalist gun and grenade attack on another IRA funeral, an attack which resulted in three deaths. The priest pictured praying over the dead corporal those few days later

165

became a very important player in that long and painful search for peace.

Now, the hope must be that the peace will hold but there are difficult times ahead in terms of trying to find political agreement. In the course of the past twenty-five years there have been numerous demands for peace – demands which came from the British, Irish and United States governments, from politicians on both sides of the Irish border, from the churches and from various peace movements. Pope John Paul II also appealed for an end to the violence during his visit to Ireland in 1979. Fifteen years later came the ceasefires and the hope today is that out of Northern Ireland's dark past will come a brighter future. It is a place where people yearn for a real and lasting peace.

INDEX

169

cessation of violence
preconditition, 92
Irish People's Liberation
Organisation (IPLO), 33
Irish Republican Army (IRA), 89,
133–4, 146; *see also* ceasefire, IRA
'anti–drugs operation', 86
army convention, 162–3
Army Council, 12, 162
attacks on, 27, 37
attacks on security forces, 57, 79,
80, 85–6, 91
bombs, 52–3
British campaign, 11, 17, 19–20,
32, 39, 50, 80
British contacts revealed, 66–71
and CLMC ceasefire (1991), 21–2
and Downing Street Declaration,
74
Easter message (1993), 42
'economic targets', 25
on Hume–Adams talks, 56–7, 61–2
internal debate, 83–5
killings by, 9–11, 17, 19, 23, 26,
39, 45, 53, 86, 91, 92, 104,
111–12, 135
McGuinness on, 38–9
meeting with Wilson, 39–42, 43
pub bombings, 91–2
reasons for ceasefire, 100–1
tactical reassessment, 31–2, 79–81

Jess, Mervyn, 120
John Paul II, Pope, 166

Keane, Mairead, 46
Kelly, Gerry, 46, 62
Kelly, James, 37
Kelly, Tom, 2, 4
Kerr, Alec, 150–1
Kerr, Frank, 163
King, Trevor, 104, 108

Kirkham, Tommy, 144, 149

Labour Party, Irish, 90
Lavery, Bobby, 37
Lisburn, County Antrim, 17, 112,
115, 143
Little, Ivan, 122, 160
London, 17, 20, 32, 50, 80
Londonderry, County, 23, 32, 33,
34, 37, 50, 54, 86, 120, 164
Loughgall battle, 27
Loughinisland attack, 103, 104–7,
136
loyalist paramilitaries *see* Combined
Loyalist Military Command
Loyalist Political Alliance, 102
Lundy, Alan, 37

McAuley, Richard, 34, 46, 47
McCrea, Revd William, 71
McDonald, Jim, 102, 123
McGimpsey, Michael, 76–8
McGuigan, Gerard, 33, 37
McGuinness, Martin, 11, 46, 67,
80, 84
Belfast speech, 57–8
British contacts, 59–61, 62, 64,
65–6, 69–70
on Downing Street Declaration,
81–2
interviews with, 38–9, 70–1
meets Bruce Morrison, 93
McKittrick, David, 99
McKnight, Cecil, 23
McLaughlin, Mitchel, 11, 30, 46,
110
on Downing Street Declaration,
73
McMahon, Patrick, 52
McMichael, Gary, 12, 102, 112,
117, 123, 143, 145
loyalist ceasefire statement, 125

171

Facsimiles of the 1994 ceasefire statements: IRA, 31 August, and Combined Loyalist Military Command, 13 October (Courtesy of John Harrison Photography)

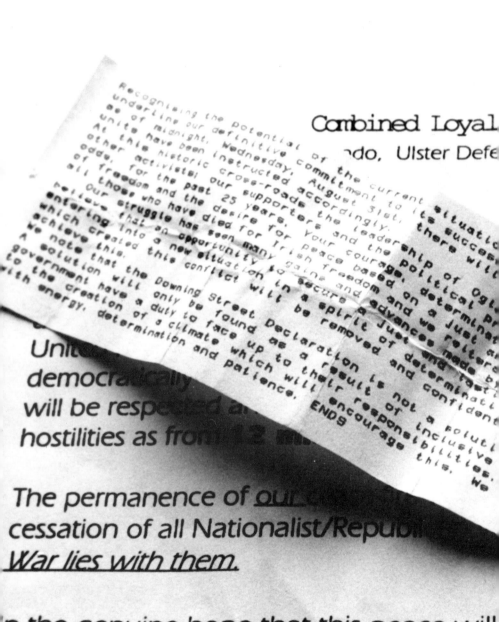